Successful Parish Leadership

Nurturing the Animated Parish

Robert G. Duch

Sheed & Ward

Acknowledgments

I would like to express my gratitude and appreciation to Bishop John McDowell who encouraged me over 20 years ago to write, and for his Foreword in this book; to Monsignor Charles Owen Rice for reading the manuscript and for his helpful suggestions; to my parents and family for their support and encouragement; to Helen Gage and Michael Burke for their many hours of clerical and computer assistance; to the Pittsburgh Diocesan Task Force for Parish Self-Study and Diocesan Office for Research and Planning for their input in the design of the Parish Survey and In-Depth Parish Self-Study; to Sr. Jean Ortenzo and Ms. Pauline Gaglia for creating the art work and for their on-going support; to Dr. Larry Whitworth for his insightful contributions; to Bob Heyer and Andy Apathy of Sheed & Ward for their assistance and willingness to publish this book; to Bob Greenleaf and his servant-leaders for inspiring me; to Avery Dulles and Myers-Briggs for informing me; to Bishop Donald Wuerl for empowering me to implement my parish leadership ideas in the Diocese of Pittsburgh through the diocesan Project for Parish Reorganization and Revitalization.

Sheed & Ward™ is a service of National Catholic Reporter Publishing Company, Inc.

Library of Congress Catalog Card Number: 89-64499

ISBN: 1-55612-353-1

Published by: Sheed & Ward
                  115 E. Armour Blvd., P.O. Box 419492
                  Kansas City, MO 64141

To order, call: (800) 333-7373

Contents

Interpretation of Cover Art

The art work on the book cover was designed by Sr. Jean Ortenzo.

The large outer circle represents the world. The cross symbolizes Christ's presence in the world. The four interlinking spheres remind us of the four "marks" of the Church. The Church is One; it is Holy; it is Catholic; and it is Apostolic. They symbolize both the parish's role and the leadership role of every baptized parishioner.

A parish that is *One* values the basic need for people to live together as brothers and sisters in one community of faith, trust, mutual caring and harmony. It is the role of parish leaders to help form that type of parish community.

A parish is *Holy* when it uplifts and transforms the lives of its members. To be holy means undergoing constant reform and conversion to gospel values. It is the role of parish leaders to teach gospel values, and lead people to holy lives.

Catholic means universal. A *Catholic* parish values the basic need to reach out to people everywhere and to serve them by fulfilling their highest priority needs. It is the role of parish leaders to be servant-leaders, serving people and leading them to God.

An *Apostolic* parish values the basic need to remain in visible apostolic continuity with the Church's own origins and to be in conformity with the institution of Christ. Apostolic parish leaders use their legitimate authority to preserve the good things of the past and present in order to give continuity and stability to the future.

The colors of silver and blue are the two colors in the art work. Silver is very malleable and ductile, and as a conductor of heat and electricity it is superior to all other metals. Blue symbolizes the qualities of being genuine and faithful.

The four interlinking spheres along with the colors silver and blue symbolize successful parish leadership in today's world.

Foreword

Vatican II touched the life of everybody from the Cardinals and Bishops in the Vatican Curia to the people in the back pews of the local Church. In the past century no other event has had such an impact on the Church and the world as did this Council. Because of the Council, neither the Church nor the world will ever be the same.

No one feels this change in the Church more than the priests, religious and lay leaders. It is they who must absorb all these changes and respond to them, not only as individuals, but also as leaders of the people. Particularly, in things presently experienced, these leaders must draw on their skills more than ever. But, of course, there is another problem. Leadership has not escaped the impact of substantial change. It can be unequivocably stated that it is no longer the time of the one pastor, one vote Church. It is a new world. The Church at every level must operate in a new and different way. The changes have raised not only new problems but new expectations as well. Not the least of these are the problems and expectations of leadership in the Church.

Father Duch, in his book *Successful Parish Leadership*, deals in depth with this subject of the need for a new kind of leadership for today's and tomorrow's Church. He makes it very clear that he is not talking about the Divine element in the Church but only the human element. It is not a discussion about faith and morals, rather it is a concern with the human organization of the Church and its operational procedures. He writes about revitalizing, restructuring, renewing and refreshing the Church in this age of great change and expectations. As such, Father Duch's work is a direct response to the Bishops' Letter of 1987, *A Sheperd's Care*. In that document the bishops of the United States challenged all of us to consider new organizational structures and more creative leadership styles for the Church in the United States. Father Duch does this.

The author presents a new concept of leadership for the Church. This presentation moves the Church from the one vote, one decision-maker type of leadership to a team leadership concept. No one person, he writes, has all the talents necessary to make leadership work in today's Church. Hence, the team approach which he proposes involves pooling the talents of many and directing them toward a plan of action which will produce solid results in a changing world. The role of the pastor, religious and lay leaders in this effort becomes significantly more important than it ever has been. It becomes a new and different role. It also becomes a significantly more difficult one.

To show the way to leaders the author gives his own paradigm for successful leadership in a Church that is characterized by the changing look of people and parishes. This original paradigm is worthy of careful examination and the present book gives an in-depth study of its many implications. Reflections on Spirit, synergistic leaders, guiding vision, shared power, and a plan of action are carefully made and are worthy of thoughtful study. The reader will gain many new and meaningful insights from an examination of these elements of the paradigm for successful leadership.

Anyone who is interested in a thoughtful response to the Bishops' challenging *A Shepherd's Care* should read this book carefully and in particular should study the very creative and very clearly presented paradigm for successful parish leadership.

+ John B. McDowell, D.D., Ph.D.
Auxilary Bishop of Pittsburgh

Introduction

Throughout this book we will draw upon sociology, psychology, ecclesiology, church documents, research on excellent corporations, and research on effective schools to make our case. Our case is that in view of a rapidly changing culture and society Catholic parishes are in need of:

1) new organizational structures;
2) new leadership styles;
3) a paradigm to guide parish leaders in reorganizing and leading their parishes to new life.

Because of the complex web of change, doubt, conflict and contradiction that exists in our society, many individual parish leaders and the parish as a communal leader feel a "loss of efficacy," i.e., the ability to make positive differences in the lives of people. For a parish to make a postive difference parish leaders should look realistically at the *organizational aspect* and *leadership aspect* of their parish.

A realistic look at reorganization and leadership is the key for successful needed change in parishes. And, we emphasize the work "realistic." Realistic means that individual leaders and organizations do not always operate in a logical, sensitive and rational world. In actual fact, individual parish leaders and the communal parish may think, feel and act in ways that are illogical, insensitive and irrational. We believe that our new paradigm builds on this realistic foundation. It suggests strategies that can animate a parish to make a positive difference in the lives of people.

Let's look at some of the common unrealistic assumptions that people have about the human organization and leadership of the Church. Then, let's compare these assumptions with realistic ones that are needed in order to reorganize our parishes and animate them with the spirit of Christ.

Unrealistic Assumptions	Realistic Assumptions
1. The organization & structure of the church cannot change. It has crystalized.	The organization & structure of the church can change. It is fluid.
2. Parishes are guided by one vision and a single set of values and goals.	Parishes are guided by several types of vision & several sets of values and goals.
3. Power is and must be established at the top.	Power is shared throughout the parish.
4. Decision-making in parishes is a logical problem-solving process with one best solution for everyone.	Decision-making in parishes should be a consensus-seeking process so that solutions can satisfy a number of people.
5. The present parish structure must be maintained at all costs.	Some of the parishes must be reorganized and revitalized.
6. Parishioners will support change that is imposed on them in a rational plan.	Parishioners will support change which flows through a participative change process.

Diocesan and parish leaders who continue to hold on to outmoded, unrealistic assumptions about organization and leadership will be sadly disappointed in the unwillingness of people to accept their type of change effort. They will be discouraged by the creation of poor morale among the people directly affected by the unrealistic change process. On the other hand, while it is impossible to please everyone completely, a realistic change process which includes envisioning, empowering, synergizing and enspiriting will help minimize disastrous consequences. A realistic, participative process is the best bet for leading parishes and parishioners to new life.

At this point in the change process we are not thinking about the quality of spiritual life, as important as that is, but about changing organizational and leadership behavior which has a direct impact on the quality of spiritual life in a parish. A parish leadership-team approach is recommended for developing realistic plans of action for animating parishes.

Both the realistic and unrealistic schools of organizational thought endorse the process of organizational goal setting. Both admit that the Church and the parish have a primary mission: to build the kingdom of God. However, they go their separate ways when they translate the same mission statement into goals, objectives and strategies, i.e., a plan of action. For instance, the diocese may have a long list of diocesan goals which is a part of the official Church policy; individual parishes may have their own list based on their immediate needs; parish leaders within the same parish may have their list of goals; parish council committees may have their list, etc. The key, in our realistic change model, is to build parish leadership teams whose members have diverse and complementary skills and talents. It is their responsibility to develop parish action plans that fulfill a variety of legitimate goals and needs, as long as the parish adheres to the overall primary mission of the Church. The realistic approach maintains that even conflicting goals can be fulfilled at different times. Clarifying and redeveloping goals is a never ending process for the realistic organization.

The unrealistic approach, in organizing and leading, is for competing forces to battle and fight to impose their goals, objectives and strategies on someone else. Often, a "blue ribbon" committee with prestige and power in the community is selected to work within the power structure to win the battle. If that approach does not work, official policies are mandated. This is your classic, confrontational, "nobody wins" approach, or somebody has to win at the expense of someone else.

Since we do live in a rapidly changing world, there are rapidly changing goals of organizational life. The realistic parish admits that these organizational goals can be multiple, ambiguous, conflicting, competing and ever changing. Our Leadership Paradigm is founded on realistic assumptions and helps leaders (both the parish as a corporate leader and individual leaders) formulate action plans.

We believe that our Leadership Paradigm is the glue that holds together the reorganization and leadership actions of a parish which wants to animate its people with the spirit of Christ. We believe that the paradigm creates unity out of diversity. The Paradigm for Leadership is a model of integration. It integrates, i.e., brings together, all of the disparate and distinct components of organizational leadership and makes them into a coherent whole. The Church, as a corporate person and leader, must lead with this type of integrity.

Individual Church leaders must also have a similar human trait of integrity. To have personal integrity

> means to deal with the many challenges, problems, temptations, and possibilities of professional and personal life from a central point of view that integrates values, intention, and action so that, while the specific actions of the person of integrity may sometimes be hard to predict, the central core, intent, and general effectiveness of those actions are always predictable. The person's actions are coherent. . . . To say that an organization has integrity is to say that it is put together well, solid, and unshakable, with all components working in concert, and that it keeps its promises. . . . However, at the same time, the integrated organization remains . . . internally flexible. . . . When spoken of in this way, the organization begins to take on human characteristics. Just as out of the complex integrated systems that make up a human being comes a unified impression of that person, so an integrated organization . . . takes on character. (1)

The communal Church and individual Church leaders must act with integrity. *A Paradigm for Church Leadership* can guide individual leaders and the communal Church to lead predictably, coherently and lovingly; and, both will take on character, the character of Jesus, our Lord and Leader.

Perhaps McKenzie said it best when he spoke about what it takes to be a Christian and a Christian leader:

> . . . the leadership of a Christian, like the rest of his/her life, will be motivated by the principle which motivates all Christians: love. Leadership will be an act of love as any other act in the life of a Christian. . . . If one has learned what it is to be a Christian, one has learned what it is to be a leader in the Christian community. (2)

1

There Is a Need for Animating Parishes

Twenty years after Vatican Council II the National Conference of Catholic Bishops (NCCB) reviewed some of the significant changes that occurred since Vatican II and listed them along with their thoughtful responses in a published document: *A Shepherd's Care: Reflections on the Changing Role of Pastor*. In this recent document (1987) the bishops are asking us to consider new organizational structures and leadership styles for tomorrow's Church in the United States. In addition to the bishops' statements many religious, lay and clerical leaders are calling for new Church models, new types of leadership, new styles of pastoring and the recognition and synergistic use of the charisms of all the baptized in revitalizing and reorganizing parishes and dioceses. While the organizational structures are being reshaped, the people in our parishes must be personally, professionally and spiritually renewed and refreshed. The bishops are asking Catholic parishes to change in their structural forms so that they may be more effective in fulfilling the needs of parishioners and nonparishioners in a rapidly changing society. It should be noted that they are not asking parishes to change their fundamental mission and purpose for existence.

There was a time, not long ago, when society was relatively stable and changes seemed to occur only occasionally. Value systems and institutions were also stable. They were almost always accepted and supported. Structures of authority were rarely criticized. Society and its institutions, including the institution of the Church, were rarely challenged or questioned. Many contemporary leaders of present day institutions may yearn for the stable and predictable days of yesteryear.

1

However, our perception of the past may only appear as "Camelot" compared to today's rapidly changing and complex world. Nevertheless, we do live in this changing world and in a Church that continues to evolve. Much is asked of the Church, its leaders and followers. We are asked to expand our services to diverse and increasing numbers of constituencies and causes, while being directly affected by dwindling human and financial resources.

For dioceses, parishes, parishioners and pastors to survive and thrive means that we cannot become dormant, burned-out, bored-out or irrelevant. We must form the future of our parishes by dreaming of what can be, by revitalizing our own spirit, by empowering each person to help develop workable plans of action for on-going reorganization development and continuing self-renewal.

To survive and thrive may mean that we must maintain some of our present parish structures. Or, it may mean that we must change other parish structures. It may also mean that we must rethink our assumptions about what "parish" means in today's complex, ever-changing world. In short, what is needed is *planned* parish growth and change.

A review of the bishops' document indicates that when Pope John XXIII convoked Vatican Council II he initiated "an ambitious program of renewal that was to affect every aspect of Church life."[1] The response to this call for universal Church renewal has resulted in 20 years of on-going change in the Church.

The first major shift was and is the changing roles of priestly leadership. The bishops are quick to point out that it is the *manner* in which pastoral functions are carried out that is changing. In addition, the needs of parishioners have changed. Because of these changes, pastors need to learn new organizational skills in order to be effective administrative leaders. Pastors must also become community leaders. "The pastor's task is not limited to individual care of the faithful. It extends by right also to the formation of a genuine Christian community."[2] Pastors must be spiritual leaders of community worship and prayer, and must promote renewed spirituality. In other words, effective leadership is required in a community setting.

Changes have occurred in the ministry of teaching. The ministry of teaching has expanded from a focus on Catholic school teaching to more diversified and more specialized education programs based on collaborative approaches between pastors and religious education personnel. Collaborative leadership practices are stressed.

Significant changes in demography and society have changed the pastoral needs of many parishes. Pastors are expected to possess competencies in counselling the married, the separated, divorced, widowed, single, young, senior citizens, gays, unemployed, the professional, and the list is endless. The diversity of people with their many different needs has created a parish situation which is complex at best and virtually impossible at worst.

After having reviewed the above pastoral situation, the Committee on Priestly Life and Ministry concluded that:

1. pastors must learn a number of skills and competencies that are relevant to a specific specialized ministry;

2. ". . . not all priests have the ability or the desire to exercise pastoral leadership as pastors. The role of the priest and the role of the pastor, while overlapping, are not the same."[3]

The second major shift that has occurred since Vatican II is in the changing relationships of pastors to bishops, fellow priests and to parishioners. There seems to be more of a personal relationship between bishops and priests. Parishioners are asking to participate in the authority structure and decision-making processes of the parish. Excellence and quality are demanded. Team ministry, collaboration, becoming more human, coordinating the charisms of a parish team—these are the expectations and realities that have surfaced and changed the role of priests, laity and bishops in the United States.

The bishops then address the changing environmental settings of parishes which create distinctive features of each parish's life and the distinctive role of the pastor. The environment defines the potential and limits of each community. They suggest that parish mission statements could help parishioners envision how their parish is unique in its particular mission.

Parish life is "conditioned, to some extent, by the setting the diocese creates through its structures, policies and programs."[4] And, of course, the Universal Church impacts the diocese and the parish.

Even spirituality and morale is changing according to the U.S. bishops. Spirituality is more diversified. Morale, unfortunately, is low and must be revitalized.

Since Vatican Council II several different and, at times, overlapping kinds of pastoring have evolved, and continue to evolve. The pastor's roles, among others, are:

1. Proclaimer of God's word. He preaches, teaches, leads prayer and is the spiritual guide for the people within a community.

2. Leader of worship. He presides at Eucharist and, among planners and other ministers is the chief liturgist in a community setting.

3. Builder of the community. He is the "coordinator of the community's gifts."[5] He must take the time to identify the charisms and talents of people, build synergistic teams, interlink and overlap the teams, and promote consensus decision-making through collaboration, interdependence and cooperative team efforts.

4. Steward of the community's resources. The complexity of the pastor's roles demands a variety of skills. Nevertheless, good order and wise administration go together. In view of the many demands, pastors will need active support systems.

The Future: The Challenge to Continue

Change will be an ever-present, never-ending, on-going fact of future life. However, by identifying future trends and wisely making future projections, parishes and dioceses can plan to meet the needs and demands of the people (parishioners, clergy and religious) while fulfilling the expectations of the Church. The future of the Church can be shaped also "by a series of choices based on values and beliefs that are shared and actively promoted."[6]

There are three distinct but interrelated trends that are causing "new patterns of parish life."[7] They are all a part of our organic system in which a change in one component impacts all of the other components.

1. The Trend: The changing profile of the American parish

   i)   Migration in the United States will continue.

   ii)   Younger Catholics are different from older Catholics.

   iii)   The Catholic population is getting older.

   iv)   The better educated Catholic has developed a spirit of "selected compliance" in regard to Mass attendance and their response to the Church's teachings on sexual ethics, birth control and divorce.

The Challenge: Evangelization and Pastoral Service

Parishes and dioceses will challenge all of the baptized to respond creatively to the changes. Clustering of parishes may be one response. As population centers shift, more painful adjustments might be required. Parishioners in rapid growth parishes will have greater opportunities to share their charisms in team-leadership approaches and in participative problem-solving and decision-making. Ethnic parishes will study their sense of purpose and mission. A growing senior citizen community will need expanded attention. There is a changing attitude about parish affiliation. Welcoming back people to the Church will be encouraged. Involving the youth in the spiritual and worship life of the parish will be addressed. The "service model" of parish and diocese is still needed. The "evangelical model" and other models or types of Church will be needed as well.

2. The Trend: Changing Resources for Parish Staffing

There is and will be an on-going decline in numbers of priests and religious men and women.

The Challenge: Continued Adjustment to New Resources

Intensified approaches are needed to recruit men for the priesthood, and men and women for the religious life. On-going training programs for priests in parish and pastoral ministries will be needed to fulfill new pastoral roles and functions in the community. Deacons, lay ministers and lay people will participate more fully in the life of the parish and diocese. Formation programs to help develop lay leadership must be established.

3. The Trend: Changes in Parish Status and Leadership Structures

Because of the first two trends some parishes may close; others may become mission churches; still others may merge or cluster with neighboring parishes. Moreover, creative people may be inspired by the Holy Spirit to create structures that we have not yet thought about.

The Challenge: Leading the Community to New Life

The above changes will precipitate any outpouring of varied emotions: sadness, anger, frustration and abandonment, even though there is a great need for reorganization and new life structures. People will experience the life—dying—death—new life cycle in some parishes.

Parish communities simply do not want to die. It is possible, however, to assist members of a community to come to a realistic assessment of their limitations and their need to regroup in relationship to other parish communities. Using an orderly process is tedious and takes time, but it is far preferable to arbitrary decision making.[8]

An Orderly Process for Change

An orderly process can be best achieved by using a conceptual framework which guides and helps parish and diocesan leaders to determine what trends, problems and challenges are critical, and how to analyze them and deal with them. It would suggest to parish leaders what specific actions should be taken.

An orderly change process must answer four questions:

1. What are the facts of the present situation?
2. What are the possibilities for the future?
3. What is the logical plan of action?
4. What effects will this plan have on people?

The conceptual framework that we will use is called: *A Paradigm for Church Leadership.* It is a theoretical model that addresses the above four questions and *leads* persons, especially teams of persons, and corporate persons (e.g., a parish, a diocese) to accomplish efficient, effective, affective and creative change and growth.

In short, a "change model" is needed for Reorganization Development of parishes and for Leadership Development of individuals in the parish. In developing both, the parish and the individual, a parish will become more effective in accomplishing the mission of the Church and in meeting the changing needs of its parishioners.

Reorganization Development is the process undertaken by the diocese and each parish to study itself, to envision the future of the parish, and to make their dreams a reality. Reorganization can provide new realistic organizational structures for parishioners in helping them fulfill their individual needs, and for parishes in helping them fulfill their expectations.

Leadership Development is a staff development process designed to foster individual and communal growth for laity, religious and clergy in parishes. Through a personal growth process they can become parish leaders. They will learn how to form a caring community, inform the community about the gospels, transform individual members into loving Christians, and reform what needs to be changed.

Reorganization development and leadership development cannot be viewed as separate processes. Both are necessary for optimum growth and successful change. They are complementary processes. The possibility for effective change without one or the other is significantly decreased. They must be overlapping and concurrent processes. Strategies used in one context can be transferred to the other when it is appropriate to do so. Both processes are facilitated through a synergistic action plan which includes: team building based on complementary charisms, envisioning the future, enspiriting people with values, empowering the laity, communicating effectively, developing and enacting parish plans of action, and supervising people and evaluating progress.

We are talking about parishes and parishioners changing and growing. And, when we address such a topic we must not forget that many people have difficulty in coping with change. For these reasons we will take time now to look at change and how it affects people.

How Change Affects People

Change is an on-going aspect of life. Conception leads to birth, to infancy, to childhood, to adolescence, to adulthood, to middle-age, to old-age and the final change is made to new life after death. In Arnold Toynbee's view, change is a cyclical process of genesis, growth, breakdown and disintegration leading to a new genesis. If we were to apply this view to today's Church we might agree that we are caught between the period of disintegration and a new genesis. If we were to think that we were in a disintegrative period without thinking about a rebirth or a re-formation, we would have little hope for the future. However, when we think about the cyclical nature of change in nature and in the world events of history we have hope for better things to come in a new genesis for ourselves, for society and for our Church which includes our parishes.

We must heed the words of John Naisbitt in his book, *Megatrends*, so that our Church does not go the way of the dinosaur.

> There are cities and companies, unions and political parties [plus our parishes and Church] in this country that are like dinosaurs waiting for the weather to change. The weather is

not going to change. The very ground is shifting beneath us. And what is called for is nothing less than all of us reconceptualizing our roles.[9]

We cannot wait for external circumstances to change. We must proactively create change. We must form the future for our Church, our parishes, and for our personal selves. We must take leadership for planned change.

First, we must recognize the need for change. We are trying our best throughout this book to indicate the reasons for change. Secondly, we must recognize the fact that some people exhibit unhealthy behavior when change faces them. Thirdly, we will attempt to show how healthy change can occur.

Since we believe that we have adequately made our case for needed change, we will go on to the second point. It is commonly held that there are four unhealthy responses to change: disabling denial, immobilizing anxiety, pathological grieving, and numbing rigidity.

Denial is probably the oldest defense against change. It can diminish the quality of life. It holds onto antiquated systems. It unconsciously fights against growth and development. It does not permit a person to take risks. It can help people deny the very existence of problems to be solved and challenges to be met.

Immobilizing anxiety means that persons and institutions are paralyzed because they are not able to make decisions, are afraid to make decisions, or for one reason or another simply cannot take action. Lack of action produces stagnation, frustration, demoralization and immobilization.

Some people respond to change with pathological grieving. They feel that the change will render their lives meaningless and worthless. A sense of futility and despondency takes over. This may occur, for instance, when people move out of an inner city parish to a suburban parish and the inner city parish is left with few parishioners and few resources. Grieving over the loss will not solve their problems. Unfortunately, through pathological grieving these people can stubbornly refuse to consider new options which can bring about new life, new genesis.

Rigidity is the opposite of flexibility. Persons or institutions believe that they can control people and prevent any changes by devising tight systems of external controls. When leaders demand movement back to the basics, fundamentalism, legalism and tighter restrictions, freedom is threatened and a rigid system of control is suggested. They believe that they can eliminate all anxiety that change may produce by taking a rigid stance against change.

On the other hand, there are four healthy responses to change: understanding the situation, maintaining appropriate levels of controlled anxiety, wholesome grieving, and establishing sound ways of monitoring our responses to change.

When we are able to identify and clarify what is changing, how and why it is changing, how we are being affected by the change, and what the results of the change might be, we are using a healthy process for handling change in our lives. We are able to understand what is happening.

Anxiety can be a healthy response to change as long as we maintain our anxiety at appropriate levels. Anxiety and frustration can be the means to lead us to better things and more creative situations. Appropriate levels of anxiety help us grow.

When things change, we gain something and we lose something. Consequently, we suffer a sense of loss. The healthy process of grieving helps free us from the past and our attachments to it.

> It is not a denial of the past. Healthy grieving recognizes the beauty of the past and realizes that it was only part of what we now know. At the same time, in grieving over the past we are sharply aware that what is known today will be let go of tomorrow. Grieving is a continual reminder to us of our participation in ongoing transformation and conversion.[10]

Finally, since change is a daily occurrence with some changes being major ones in our lives, we need to use different responses at different times. We do this by monitoring the situation and determining what the appropriate response is at this particular time.

In our fast changing world, there are persons who may feel unable, incompetent and actually afraid to consider certain changes in their lives. They can be helped, not by making decisions for them which gives them the feeling that they are losing control of their lives, but rather by giving them as much control as possible in making decisions that directly affect their lives. We must create a climate conducive for needed change by establishing supportive networks and personal relationships based on accurate knowledge, genuine caring, and mutual respect and responsibility. Only in this type of climate can change lead to a new genesis. Only in this type of loving climate can we renew ourselves, and reorganize and revitalize our parishes. Only in this type of climate can parish leaders lead effectively.

N.B.: For additional readings on:

1. How Parish Leaders Can Facilitate Change,
   see Appendix D.

2. Adult Learning and the Process of Change
   see Appendix E.

Is There a Leadership Crisis in Our Changing Society?

For American Catholics certain types of leaders in a pluralistic society create tensions, and demand new study and consideration in light of the diversity of values in our culture and in view of the trends that point to needed change. Church leaders are being asked to be sensitive to the variety of life styles and values that are important to people. They must have the capacity to lead their parishioners toward understanding rapidly changing contemporary life and how to live with complexity, ambiguity and daily cultural conflict based on gospel values.

Robert Greenleaf, author of *Servant Leadership* and numerous articles about institutions and their leaders, describes how society has changed in the past century. He points his finger at a leadership crisis which has caused serious deficiencies in the quality of our institutions, including the

Church. Greenleaf believes that the leadership crisis of our times is without precedent.

> People have been poorly served by their leaders before; but in the past one hundred years we have moved from a society comprised largely of artisans and farmers with a few merchants and professionals, and with small government, to widespread involvement with a vast array of institutions— often large, complex, powerful, impersonal, not always competent, sometimes corrupt. Nothing like it before has happened in our history. This recent experience with institutions may have brought a new awareness of serious deficiencies in the quality of our common life that are clearly traceable to leadership failures. Some of these lacks have become so painful to bear that leadership crisis is an apt term to describe an important aspect of our present condition.[11]

Another well known and respected authority on leadership, Warren G. Bennis, corroborates Greenleaf's thoughts.

> We have the important emergence of a Roosevelt-Keynes revolution, the new politics of multiple advocacy, new dependencies, new constituencies, new regulatory controls, new values. And how do our endangered species, the leaders, cope with these new complications and entanglements? For the most part, they do not; that is, they are neither coping nor leading. One reason, I fear, is that many of us misconceive what leadership is about. Leading does not mean managing; the difference between the two is crucial. I know many institutions that are very well managed and very poorly led. They may excel in the ability to handle the daily routine, and yet they may never ask whether the routine should be done at all. To lead, the dictionary informs us, is to go in advance of, to show the way, to influence or induce, to guide in direction, course, action, opinion. To manage means to bring about, to accomplish, to have charge of or responsibility for, to conduct.

The difference may be summarized as activities of vision and judgment versus activities of efficiency.[12]

The quality of the educational institution and its leadership is being questioned also. The scorching document, *A Nation At Risk*, not only gives a scathing report about the woeful inadequacies of public school education but also identifies school leaders as significant keys to the quality of schooling. Former U.S. Secretary of Education, Terrel Bell, recognized this problem when he remarked that the first step in improving the quality of education is to improve the quality of leadership in the schools. Our schools cannot be any better than the kind of leadership we give them.

What about the quality of leadership on Wall Street? When some of Wall Street's brightest stars were arrested in 1987 in New York for insider trading, shock waves were felt 200 miles away in Cambridge, Massachusetts, home of Harvard Business School. This is the ivy-covered cornerstone of American capitalism and the first step on the ladder of success for many aspiring entrepreneurs. Several of the Wall Street geniuses who were indicted were alumni of the prestigious school. The scandals not only embarrassed Harvard, but incited debate over the proper status of teaching values and ethical leadership in the school's curriculum.

Recent scandals and failures of government officials are numerous and painful to remember. "Watergate," "Contragate" and "Irangate" are just three incidents that revive memories of government leadership at its worst.

In the meantime, the Church is experiencing great difficulty in its ability to transmit its teaching and values to its younger members because of negative influences of a pluralistic society. Nor is the Church attracting and forming new leaders to assure an effective Church for future generations.

Avery Dulles criticizes the Church and its leadership, thereby giving us some important clues to what Church leadership should not be.

> One may say that many think of the Church as a huge, impersonal machine set over against its own members. The top officers are regarded as servants of the institution, bound by a rigid party line, and therefore inattentive to the impulses of the

Holy Spirit and unresponsive to the legitimate religious concerns of the faithful. The hierarchy, according to this view, are prisoners of the system they impose on others. Following the inbuilt logic of all large institutions, they do what makes for law and order in the Church rather than what Jesus himself would be likely to do . . . . Today, especially in the North Atlantic nations, people take a critical view of all institutions . . . . It seems almost impossible to look upon a huge bureaucracy as a loving mother, yet this, it seems, is precisely what the Church is asking them to do . . . . The laws and dogmas of the Church seem designed to control and crush rather than to nourish and satisfy the needs of the Spirit.[13]

While criticizing the Church, Dulles also suggests what Church leaders must do in order to be effective in contemporary society. Tradition must be related faithfully, yet there must be a creative response to the needs of new demands in future generations. In the future Church leaders will not be able to exert canonical penalties and ecclesiastical pressures to control their followers. Less force and more persuasion will be needed. This means that there will be increased need for dialogue and consensus. It also means that Church leaders must listen to the lead of the Holy Spirit.[14]

Greenleaf, a Quaker and an avid student of institutions, offers his insightful look at the Catholic Church in the United States.

The Catholic Church in the United States is a minority religion, but I regard it as, potentially, our largest single force for good. It fails to realize its potential for good in the society as a whole because, I believe, it is seen as predominantly a negative force. The issues on which the Church is in opposition, such as birth control, abortion, euthanasia, divorce, and communism, are specific and precisely defined, and the actions of the Church are vigorous and sustained . . . . One must oppose those things that one believes to be wrong, but one cannot lead from a predominantly negative posture. One can lead an institution or a total society only by strong, specific, sharply aimed affirmative actions . . . . Pope John XXIII's regime lifted people because an affirmative building leadership seemed to be emerging, and this gave a new hope for the world . . . . The present dilemma is: so many of the forces of good are trying to cancel out what they regard as error, and too few are attending to the quality of the institutions that dominate us all . . . . An institution enlarges and liberates.[15]

We must remind ourselves that we who are approaching the 21st century are different from men and women in other centuries; and that persons in future centuries will be different from us. Nevertheless, some of the vestiges of the outmoded Christian Church are still present and must be changed. The Church and the parish must be institutions that enable, free and empower men and women of this and every century to shape their own destiny, to seek the same freedom that men and women of past centuries have sought.

The Church still depends primarily on its bishops. Some live in the past and have become victims of the past. Some have not been able to grow and learn leadership behaviors suggested by Vatican II: collegiality, participative problem solving, shared decision making, etc. It is easier for some to remain authoritarian, legalistic, conservative, clericalist and triumphalist. We see examples of individual bishops who are fine people, yet lack creativity, imagination, courage and the charism of leadership. Some seem to depend too much on Rome instead of depending on the Holy Spirit to help build the Kingdom here on earth. "It is vital for religion to recognize the signs of the times, accept them, and give fresh life to its own structures."[16]

However, it goes without saying that more and more of our American bishops have been able to acknowledge the signs of the times, accept them and listen to the Holy Spirit. They are trying to pump new life into the present structures of the Church, and trying to restructure, revitalize and reorganize. Moreover, our United States bishops are trying to help Vatican officials understand and appreciate the healthy aspects of our American culture while being realistic about its negative features. Vatican officials are emphasizing the unchanging truths of the Church. We see signs of hope through recent dialogue between the American hierarchy and the Pope.

One of the biggest challenges for Catholics, especially Catholics who were educated in their formative years before Vatican II, was and is the impression that everything in the Church is settled, that Church teachings are unchangeable and inflexible. Then Vatican Council II occurred, and we were told that there were many things that we did not completely understand. They were puzzling and challenging times. To our surprise we were told that leadership had many shapes in the Church; that the structures of the Church had developed gradually through the centuries; that laypeople should participate in consensus decision making; that laypeople would be lectors and eucharistic ministers, etc.

We do know that no human institution can survive for very long without quality leadership. And, insofar as the Church is a huge institution in the modern world, leadership challenges exist comparable to other large institutions. However, the Church, as a leading institution, must take the lead in establishing ways to reorganize and reanimate itself. Christian leadership must be taught to all of its members since their lives are directly affected by the Church. The Church must transform current influential leaders of our American institutions into influential *Christian leaders*. The Church must teach the Christian use of power and appropriate leadership styles by its own example of leading the Church in America.

Church leaders in today's society must possess some kind of democratic legitimacy to be strong leaders. Many Catholic bishops, priests and lay leaders would be able to lead their followers more effectively if they knew how to create a base of democratic consensus for their authority. In the United States democracy and governance depend upon the consent of the governed. At the same time, legitimate authority is needed in order to prevent authoritarianism and anarchy.

As in every time and culture, the Church is always called upon to adapt to the changing needs of men and women in the Christian community. Church leaders have the responsibility to discern what needs to change and what needs to remain stable and constant. The training of Church leaders must include serious study of the history of the Church; yet, potential leaders must learn how to lead creatively in an ever and fast changing world. Church leaders are expected to be efficient managers, knowledgeable and informed executives, caring and responsive servants, leaders with the ability to enhance Christian living within the community of the Church. They must understand persons, institutions, Sacred Scripture, Jesus Christ and different models of Church in contemporary society. They must be able to scrutinize the signs of the times and the challenges of their age. They must be able to offer a Christian response which considers the needs of individuals while maintaining the integrity of the Church. Leaders must have a shared vision which people will follow. They must possess and convey a spirit which will sustain people in their quest of the vision. The power that they use is the paradox of power through weakness, life through death. It is the power of love and Christian presence. It is power received from the Holy Spirit to authentically reinterpret the gospel message for today's people. The result of this kind of Church leadership is an authentic Christian community, a building up of Christ's Church in today's culture.

In the context of what a Church leader must be, it becomes apparent that no *one* mere mortal person can be all of the above. Each person has strengths and weaknesses and some abilities to perform some leadership functions. One leader may focus on serving others, and he/she probably does that well. Another leader may focus on using legitimate authority to preserve the stability and continuity of the Church and he/she probably does that well. Or, a leader may focus on change because the signs of the times indicate "aggiornamento" is needed. Other leaders focus on strengthening the harmony and loving relationships among people in community. Each leader possesses some talents. However, no one leader possesses all of the needed talents.

One of the recommendations of this book is to suggest to parishes that they modify their present hierarchical leadership styles and reconsider the style used in early Christianity: "Primus inter pares" (first among equals). This is the leadership style where the leader is "first" but not the "chief at the top." There is a subtle difference, shifting from the pyramidal structure to a team of equals with a "first." In its pure form the College of Bishops with the Pope as head (first) is the best example of this form of leadership.

Many American, European and Japanese corporations have turned to this style of leadership with its hallmark being participative decision-making.

> Decision making by consensus has been the subject of a great deal of research in Europe and the United States over the past twenty years, and the evidence strongly suggests that a consensus approach yields more creative decisions and more effective implementation than does individual decision making.[17]

If capitalistic corporations can trust their co-workers by empowering them to be co-responsible in making important decisions, should not the Church which teaches that the Holy Spirit makes us equal members in the Church also seek consensus in matters that directly affect its members? We are not talking about faith and morals. We are talking about the temporal concern of the Church, the human organization and its operational procedures. We are talking about revitalizing and restructuring. We are also talking about being renewed, refreshed and having our capabilities regenerated.

A Church which claims that all its members are led by the Holy Spirit, that all members have been freed by the blood of Christ to form their own consciences with the guidance of the Church, that members live in different cultures with different values, that it calls itself "The People Of God"—perhaps this kind of Church needs to look at itself again and then determine what kind of Church it claims to be, what it proclaims it must be in the immediate future, and what kind of leadership is needed to support its claims and proclamations.

> The Council brought us new insights . . . . We began to realize that, if she is to measure up to her own inexhaustible potentialities and the demands of an age without precedent in human history, her leaders must learn to think radically and to act with audacity. Especially was it necessary to engage in basic theological thinking. In particular, the Church must reflect upon herself, her nature and limits, her functions and her mission. Such was the business emphasized by the new Pope when he inaugurated the second session of the Council.[18]

> > Vatican II rocked the boat of the Church that was cruising along. Some people jumped overboard. Many others

weathered the storm and are still searching for a Church that can buoy them through the rapids of cultural and societal change.

In what will undoubtedly be a landmark study of the American Catholic parish, Joseph Gremillion and Jim Castilli describe some of those changes that have already occurred in our parish culture. These are some of their conclusions from *The Notre Dame Study of Catholic Life Since Vatican II:*

1. "Catholics follow Church teaching when they agree with it."[19]

2. Approximately 50% of Catholics "want to attend a parish that meets their individual needs."[20]

3. "For today's Catholics the parish is not a service station for the sacraments. They turn to the parish for Community, services, and opportunities to serve. This sense of community, expanded parish programs and services, and increased opportunity for participation are responsible for and fed by an explosion of lay-participation in parish life."[21]

4. "Catholics want more from their parishes...in terms of help with personal problems, and they want more opportunities for ecumenical and social service activity."[22]

5. ". . . in the post-Vatican II parish . . . a good social life improves a congregation's spiritual life."[23]

6. there is an "emphasis in American congregations on parish renewal."[24]

7. ". . . parish vitality is related to a sense of community . . . ."[25]

8. ". . . Vatican II's 'community organization' has been an overwhelming success in the United States."[26]

2

Typology Is Used to Analyze the Institution of the Church and Individual Persons in the Church

The world and its institutions, including the institution of the Church, have witnessed and experienced many changes since Vatican Council II in the 1960's. The image of the Church portrayed by the Council as People of God, has been portrayed recently as Healer, and even more recently as the "Disciple Church." These recent images of the Church can be added to a lengthy list of past models, such as: mystical body, military model, political model, holy mother church, monastic model, moral entity, herald, institutional model, body of Christ, experiential model, sacramental model, and others. Images are vitally important to the Church because we live by myth and symbol. "All of man's contacts with grace or revelation, if they do not inevitably originate in symbol, end there."[1]

Images are helpful in understanding the vision of the Church and they provide an integrating spirit which bonds its members into a faith community. They give us purpose and a special esprit-de-corps. They permeate our liturgical celebrations and give us content for preaching and living. They provide a symbolism which is necessary to any human institution.

Dulles uses the science of typology to study the various images of Church. He says that:

> basic types reflect distinctive mind-sets that become manifest in a given theologian's way of handling all the problems to which he addresses himself . . . . The method of models or types can have great value in helping people to get beyond the limitations of their own particular outlook, and to enter into fruitful conversation with others having a fundamentally different mentality . . . . The method of typology . . . should help to foster the kind of pluralism that heals and unifies, rather than a pluralism that divides and destroys.[2]

The Church relies on images to help people understand abstract theological and scriptural ideas. Cleansing water, a glowing Easter candle in a dark church, a sign of the cross, genuflections, a kiss of peace during the liturgy, the Sacred Heart, the Lamb of God and many other symbols and images complement each other and give us a fuller, more comprehensive view of the Church. In themselves they are limiting, but they also mutually qualify each other.

When a person prefers one type or image to another, valuable clues are given in regard to what type of Church that person is attracted. The preference can also indicate certain behavior patterns as Church leader or Church members. For instance, the person who prefers to focus on the Church as a Servant Church probably wants the Church to become more involved in helping the poor, the downtrodden, etc. Whereas, the person who focuses on the Church as the People of God prefers that Church leaders and followers live in peace and harmony, and lead the world toward international peace. These basic mind-sets become manifest in the way people behave, and in that sense they can "predict" certain patterns of behavior.

Typological approaches can be used to understand the basic types of Church and basic personality-types. This dual approach gives birth to a new paradigm: *A Paradigm for Church Leadership.*

The ancient creeds, based on certain scriptural passages, described the Church as One, Holy, Catholic and Apostolic. Church-going Catholics attest to these *four types of Church* everytime they recite the Nicene Creed. These four adjectives are used in fundamental theology as the four "marks" of the Church, and they are intrinsically tied to the fundamental concept of Church. Each mark creates a distinctive mind set and gives rise to a specific type or model of Church. And, usually Catholics view the Church in terms of their parish.

A spirit is created within the parish, a spirit which binds people together in a characteristically distinctive institution. This spirit also becomes an energizing mood which gives vitality to the parish. Parishioners try to be one. They try to be holy. They try to be apostolic and catholic.

A typological approach to human personality purports that there are *four basic patterns of human behavior*. This is a result of the work of Carl Jung who identified categories of psychological-types. Isabel Briggs Myers extended his work through her life long efforts. In Jung's theory, there are four mental processes which categorize all conscious mental activity. Sensing and intuition are the two processes of perception. Thinking and feeling are the two processes of judgment. The four basic patterns give us clues about a person's mental habits: what interests them, what they focus on, what their preferences are, what they care about.

The hypothesis presented here is that specific personality types are attracted spontaneously to specific types of Church; and, that the two merge into a specific leadership style and followership style. Specific leaders give vitality to a specific type of Church: one or holy or catholic or apostolic. They usually focus on and emphasize one or two types but not all types or models. That is, they prefer one model of Church to another.

For our purposes in this book, we must also inform our readers that we are examining the human institution of the Church, not the divine institution. Hans Küng makes the distinction very clear. He sees Church as "Ekklesia" and "Basileia."[3]

EKKLESIA	BASILEIA
1. is a pilgrimage;	1. is the final glory;
2. embraces sinners and the righteous	2. is the kingdom of the righteous & saints;
3. grows from below, can be organized; is the product of development and progress and dialectic; in short, is definitely the work of man.	3. comes from above, is an unprepared action, an incalculable event; in short, is definitely the work of God.
4. human institution.	4. divine institution.

It is the human side of the Church to which this book addresses itself. We will explore the human institution, the human persons in the institution and its human leaders. The purpose of the exploration is to help us understand more intimately the wonderful and beautiful humanity of each person, and that our understanding will lead us to a greater love of each person who has been created in the image and likeness of God. We hope to gain an understanding of how human leadership can work best for a human and divine Church.

Based on this methodology, we will analyze how parishes and dioceses can meet the challenges of the United States bishops in their pastoral letter, *A Shepherd's Care*, and make the necessary changes in revitalizing, restructuring and reorganizing parishes, and for renewing, refreshing and regenerating parishioners.

To ask people to change is asking a lot. To ask people to change the organizational/communal form of their beloved parish is asking a lot more. However, if they are empowered to use their God-given talents, if they are invited to help determine their own future, and if they are taught new leadership skills and parish reorganization strategies, they will be capable and responsible co-leaders in building God's Kingdom here on earth and in "renewing the face of the earth."

Allotting his gifts to everyone according as He will (1 Cor. 12: 11), he (the Spirit) distributes special graces among the faithful of every rank. By these gifts he makes them fit and ready to undertake the various tasks or offices advantageous for the renewal and upbuilding of the Church . . . .[4]

3

A Paradigm for Church Leadership

First of all, let us describe a paradigm. The concept of a paradigm can be likened to an aerial photograph of a town. It shows the whole town in one picture, and the individual landmarks are easily identified. The "town" and its individual persons can use the photograph as a map to lead people to specific destinations by suggesting certain routes for travel.

Our paradigm is a conceptual picture of the parish. The "parish" and its individual persons can lead people to specific destinations by suggesting certain ways of acting. Consequently, our paradigm is one of "leading," i.e., the parish is a corporate leader, and the parishioners are individual leaders. The parish and its parishioners have the responsibility to lead themselves to revitalization and reorganization. The paradigm for leadership provides them with the road map to do that.

The Paradigm presents a wholistic picture which differentiates its individual components. It also subsumes, defines and interrelates those same component parts. Within the structure of the paradigm each component is further specified.

It serves as a puzzle-solving tool. It solves the puzzle of how parish leaders can analyze the present situation of parishes and then guide them in designing an orderly process for change. The paradigm helps leaders analyze the whole picture through each of its parts. The paradigm is prophetic because it is a predictive tool which has the capacity to help us understand how an individual leader or an institution will probably act, and how they can lead most effectively. It is a map which indicates the best route for leaders and parishes to take.

Our paradigm is a shift from the hierarchical, top man, one decision-maker leadership paradigm of the past and present. Our paradigm shift offers a significant change in thinking, feeling and acting as Church leaders at this point in the history of a parish and diocese. As all paradigms intend to do, this too is a new way of looking at the world of our parishes, dioceses and their leaders. Changes suggested by new paradigms have been and will continue to be judged harshly by some critics. Nevertheless, paradigm shifts have occurred throughout history and will continue to occur in the future.

For instance, a paradigm shift occurred with the signing of the Magna Carta (1215). It was a bill of rights for English lords, guaranteeing them their rights and privileges. This evolved into individual liberty for all, and eventually evolved into the French and American revolutions.

In the 18th century philosophers stressed the importance of human reasoning and rejected everything that could not be proved by reason. The result was that, from this time on, religion occupied a secondary position in the lives of many people. This model of living lasted into the 20th century.

Imperialism, colonialism, communism and capitalism are examples of paradigm shifts. The Industrial Revolution gave rise to inventions for the benefit of society's material progress. At the same time, it created problems: exploitation of the uneducated masses of people who were not prepared for the problems that an industrial economy forced upon them. Populations shifted from farms to overpopulated cities. New ways of thinking and acting were necessary.

A most significant change was a change of "world view." Darwin's *On The Origin of Species and The Descent of Man* stated the revolutionary idea that living things, including people, were not the product of an immediate creation by God. Instead, they were the result of evolution. This caused a violent storm of protest among Catholics and Protestants alike. However, Chardin tried to demonstrate that science and religion are twin endeavors helping men and women to understand themselves as persons in the material world. He showed that scientific discoveries help people appreciate more fully the beauty of creation (*The Phenomenon of Man*). Faced with a new world view (an evolutionary view as distinct from a static view), Christians could see Christ as the center of and reason for God's creative dynamic. The heart of the Christian message was not changed, only its human view was changed.

Evolution is another word for the creative dynamism of God, who is constantly creating—making all things new. This new way of looking at the world, a new paradigm or model, resulted in profound changes in the Catholic Church and culminated in Vatican Council II. Pope John XXIII called the bishops together to update the Church in the world because he believed that the Church had been shutting itself off from the mainstream of civilization and was becoming less influential in the lives of its members. A significant number of critics are renewing the same criticism today. That is, many of our parishes and dioceses are shutting themselves off from the mainstream of local communities. They are becoming less and less influential in the lives of their parishioners.

The Council rejected the image of the Church which "pictured" itself as the guardian of the faith and the depository of truth. The new picture or paradigm was "The New People Of God," an historical living reality of the saving event of Christ. The Vatican II bishops created a new image, a new model, a new paradigm which resulted in a new world view, a new way of thinking, feeling and acting. It gave leaders and followers in the Church a new flexibility, freedom and personal responsibility.

The Western Church began to express its religious freedom with its own style and corporate identity. The National Council of Bishops was founded in the United States. In fact and interestingly enough, Vatican II urged all bishops of every region to adopt the "American Scheme."

The Church was manifesting its unity within its diversity, and not without difficulty. However, some people were slow to accept diverse cultural expressions of faith. The advice of Pope John XXIII was: "In incidentals let us have diversity, in essentials let us have unity, but in all let there be charity."

Understanding Jesus's presence in the world through the Church requires a new paradigm for each cultural shift. The paradigm of the Secular State was necessary and used for centuries by the Church. The paradigm of the Mystical Body was used in 1943 and displaced the paradigm of the Perfect Society. Vatican II proposed People of God. Servant or Healer is being suggested for a world that is concerned about justice and peace for all people in a fast shrinking global community. Avery Dulles is suggesting that we are all disciples of the Lord, and that the Church paradigm is a "Disciple Church."

Each age shows how it understands the Christ-event in its own time. Paradigms are pictures of that understanding. When men and women know more about themselves and the Church, and the world in which they live, they will be able to formulate new answers to relevant questions of their times.

The bishops of the United States are asking those relevant questions about today's Church in their pastoral, *A Shepherd's Care*. They list the demographic and societal trends and ask us to respond to the attendant challenges. Two of the key strategies in meeting their challenges are to design an orderly process and to develop effective parish leaders to implement it skillfully and sensitively.

Who are effective leaders? Synergistic leaders are effective leaders. What is synergistic (synergy)? In biology, it is the combined and correlated organs which produce united action. In medicine, it is the correlation or concurrence of action between different drugs in health or disease. In theology, it is the doctrine that human effort cooperates with divine grace in the salvation of the soul.

For our purposes, synergistic leaders are persons who acknowledge the charisms (talents and gifts) that they and others possess. They use their own charisms for the good of the community. They empower others to use their charisms in a team-leadership approach. This produces a united action for the common good of the parish and the diocese: the Church which is "The People of God." In *A Shepherd's Care*, the U.S. bishops point out the need for the leader to be the coordinator of the community's charisms. In other words, to coordinate the many and diverse talents of parishioners in the parish community is to lead synergistically.

Human nature being what it is, a person prefers to use and is very good at using one charism or a few at best. That is why it makes more sense to have a leadership team (first among equals) which includes a variety of leaders with a variety of complementary charisms. Their combined abilities, based on a co-equal status (with one being "first") in the parish, will produce a more caring, better serving, better managed and much more effectively led institution.

> ... surely the Christian witness of working together unceasing-ly—even if not always easily—to hasten the coming of the Kingdom stands equal to the Christian witness of the love we bear one another as a sign to the world of God's presence among us.[1]

In other words, a paradigm shift is needed from the hierarchical, one top man leadership model to a synergistic, team model if leadership is to be effective in today's and tomorrow's Church. Let me also list additional reasons for such a necessary shift.

• The framers of Vatican II teachings are still awaiting the fuller implementation of their ideas. The call for collegiality, shared decision making, the priesthood of the laity, consensus, etc. has been heard and implemented by few in the Church. Others would like to use these ideas and processes, but have not been taught how to use them appropriately.

• In the United States where democracy, pluralism and freedom of expression prevail, hierarchical structures and decision making processes must shift to more culturally accepted practices if Catholics are to feel that they are an integral part of the Church, and not second class citizens.

• Ideas proposed in best selling books, *Theory Z, Principles of Japanese Management, In Search of Excellence,* and others have been implemented in American, European and Japanese corporations with much success. Their ideas of leadership and management of corporations are similar to those proposed in Vatican II documents on the Church. Many corporations have achieved a needed paradigm shift for the leadership of their human institutions. Many of them have set a worthy example for the human leadership of the institution of the Church.

• There are definite negative features in continuing to use hierarchical leadership ideas in the operation of the Church's institutions. According to Greenleaf, some of them are the following.

> To be a lone chief atop a pyramid is abnormal and corrupting. None of us are perfect by ourselves, and all of us need the help and correcting influence of close colleagues. When someone is moved atop a pyramid, that person no longer has colleagues, only subordinates. Even the frankest and bravest of subordinates do not talk with their boss in the same way that they talk with colleagues who are equals, and normal communication patterns become warped . . . . A self protective image of omniscience often evolves from these warped and filtered communications . . . . Those persons who are atop the pyramids often suffer from a very real loneliness. They cannot be sure enough of the motives of those with whom they must deal, and they are not on the grapevine . . . . A close observation of top persons everywhere reveals the burden of indecisiveness to be much greater than the benefit of decisiveness . . . . Everywhere there is much complaining about too few leaders. We have too few because most institutions are structured so that only a few—only one at a time—can emerge . . . . The typical chief who rests uneasily atop the pyramid of any large institution is grossly overburdened. The job destroys too many of them . . . . When there is but a single chief, there is a major interruption when that person leaves . . . . and the search continues for 'the person who has everything.' And there is the inevitable disillusionment. The chosen one turns out to have feet of clay like everybody else . . . . The single chief holds too much power. Chiefs often cannot say persuasively what they would like to say because it will be taken as an order. No one else can effectively speak for the chief because the listeners rightly want to know what the chief thinks . . . . When more converges on the single chiefs than they can handle, but they must appear to be handling it alone, they most often resort to concentrated briefing and the support

of ghost writing . . . . In the end the chief becomes a performer, not a natural person . . . . The prevalence of the lone chief places a burden on the whole society because it gives control priority over leadership. It sets before the young the spectacle of an unwholesome struggle to get to the top.[2]

If the lone chief idea is no longer workable in today's institutions, what does work? To begin to answer this question we must recognize the fact that a revolution, a pradigm shift, has occurred.

In a relatively short period our society has moved from a society of individuals to a society dominated by large institutions. Many of the critics of society do not see our problems as caused by this shift . . . . As a consequence we have a crisis of institutional quality . . . . Unless the quality of large institutions can be raised, not much can be done to improve the total society.[3]

Quality of institutions and quality of leadership go hand-in-hand. The quality of our parishes and dioceses cannot be raised unless contemporary leaders (both, the parish and the individual) admit our individual shortcomings as imperfect persons and imperfect parishes in need of personal renewal and organizational revitalization. We must begin to admit our need for a supportive, interdependent, co-equal team of leaders with a "first." We must also admit the related need in some demographic areas for interdependent, interlinking and overlapping parishes within a community setting. This type of synergistic leadership will create synergistic parishes and dioceses, and a network of people united in action. Consequently, the quality of Church institutions will be raised significantly.

A new paradigm could guide parish leadership teams in an orderly process for studying the quality of their parish, the dreams they have for their parish, the strengths and weaknesses of their parish, and what plans of action must be taken to assure quality and excellence of a future parish community.

Our paradigm has a dual perspective. It can help individual persons analyze and understand themselves as leaders, and provide clues about how and why they act in specific ways. The paradigm also helps the parish and diocese (corporate leaders) analyze themselves. It helps them understand how they impact people. It gives them insights into what should be retained, developed or changed in the institution to assure quality and excellence.

To repeat, the paradigm refers to personal leadership of individuals and to the corporate leadership of an institution. In other words, a pastor may be a leader, a parish council member may be a leader, a parish may be a leader, and a diocese may be a leader. Through our paradigm we will analyze and describe what makes them leaders and suggest how they can lead effectively.

This new paradigm is analogous to an organism which has a number of interlinking parts. The parts are called elements. An element is an essential component or primary part of an organism. Air, earth, fire and water are essential elements of this planet which is a huge, complex organism. In every healthy organism all of the essential elements interrelate and compose a symmetrical whole.

Six elements constitute the healthy organism which we call

A Paradigm for Church Leadership: RSVP3

> Results
>
> Spirit
>
> Vision
>
> Person
>
> Power
>
> Plan of Action

The typological approach of our paradigm tries to *lead* individuals to self-renewal and parishes to organizational restructuring and communal revitalization.

Each element of the paradigm is composed of four basic types. There are four basic types of *Persons*: Sensing-Thinking Persons, Sensing-Feeling Persons, Intuitive-Feeling Persons, and Intuitive-Thinking Persons.

There are four basic types of *Spirit* that flow spontaneously from each corporate and individual personality-type: the Spirit of being One, the Spirit of being Holy, the Spirit of being Catholic, and the Spirit of being Apostolic.

There are four basic types of *Vision* that flow spontaneously from each type of Person and type of Spirit: the Vision of Authority, the Vision of Servant, the Vision of Community, the Vision of Prophet.

There are four basic types of *Power* that flow spontaneously from each type of Person, Spirit and Vision: the Power of Knowledge, the Power of Care, the Power of Responsibility, and the Power of Respect.

There are four basic types of *Results* that flow spontaneously from each type of Person, Spirit, Vision and Power: Information, Formation, Transformation and Re-Formation.

There are four basic types of *Plans of Action*: Efficient Plans, Effective Plans, Affective Plans, and Creative Plans.

Now we will offer our definition of "leaders," present our paradigm, and define, analyze and describe the six elements and each type of element individually and separately.

This is our definition of leaders:

LEADERS
are
synergistic
PERSONS
who animate their followers
with an energizing
SPIRIT
and a guiding
VISION
and share
POWER
to produce lasting

RESULTS
for parishioners and parishes
through a realistic
PLAN OF ACTION.

A PARADIGM FOR LEADERSHIP

PERSONS -		ST (Sensing-Thinking)	SF (Sensing-Feeling)	NF (iNtuition-Feeling)	NT (iNtuition-Thinking)
SPIRIT	=	APOSTOLIC	CATHOLIC	ONE	HOLY
VISION	=	AUTHORITY	SERVANT	COMMUNITY	PROPHET
POWER	=	KNOWLEDGE	CARE	RESPON-SIBILITY	RESPECT
RESULTS	=	INFORMING	TRANS-FORMING	FORMING	RE-FORM-ING
PLAN OF ACTION	=	EFFICIENT	EFFECTIVE	AFFECTIVE	CREATIVE

4

Leaders are Persons

> In real life the most practical advice for leaders is not to treat
> pawns like pawns, nor princes like princes, but all persons like
> persons.[1]

Pope John Paul II's visit to the United States and Canada in September,
1987, prompted many varied reactions from Catholics and Non-Catholics
alike. Some people were truly excited that the Pope would visit their city.
They welcomed the opportunity to see him in person, although that moment might be a fleeting glance of a Pope, moving quickly in his
popemobile. Nevertheless, emotions of affection and love, dislike and
hatred stirred in the hearts of people.

There were others who thought that the Pope's trip was too expensive;
that public, private and Church money expended for his visit was unwisely
spent. Matter of factly, his visit was impractical. It would have been better had the Pope stayed at the Vatican and issued some concrete edicts,
bringing law and order back to the Church.

Still others, theologians and scholars in particular, had another concern.
And that was the Pope's outlook and vision of the Catholic Church in the
United States. Their representatives met the Pope head on in debate over
key Church issues and future challenges. Theirs was an intellectual approach about tenets of the faith.

There were people waiting anxiously for Pope John Paul II to give them
a sense of mission, telling them how to continue their journey in search of
the sacred in a corrupt world. They were looking for self-actualization in
and through the Church.

Different viewpoints. Varied outlooks. A focus on different values.
Feelings were being expressed. Logical ideas were being shared. Some

people were vocal. Others were reticent. Judgments were being made very quickly by some. Others wanted to reflect on the Pope's words and, only then, try to decide how they viewed the Catholic Church and how they were to be members of that Church.

While these were exciting times for many people in the United States, the Pope's visit illustrated very clearly how different people are. Carl Jung (1923) said that people are different in fundamental ways and that these differences are good and healthy. Human beings prefer to function in different ways. Myers-Briggs, building on Jung's work, said that we have different personality-types. Each personality-type is innately and environmentally disposed to prefer certain ways of functioning over other ways.

The four sets of preferences are: 1) introversion or extraversion; 2) intuition or sensing; 3) thinking or feeling; 4) judging or perceiving. Each set contains opposite ways of acting. However, the healthy personality-type is one who is able to think logically when the situation calls for that preference to be used; and to use one's feelings when the situation calls for that particular preference to be used. When a person needs to use energy to deal with people, the extraversion preference can be used. And, when a person needs some quiet time for reflection and meditation, the healthy personality-type is able to call on and use the function of introversion.

To repeat, the healthy personality-type is the one who can use any preference when needed in order to cope and deal with the fast-changing situations of daily life.

We use a mixture of introversion/extraversion; thinking/feeling; intuition/sensing; judging/perceiving. However, each human being prefers to use, and is more comfortable in using one preference over the other in each set of preferences. We become comfortable in using our stronger or "dominant" preferences. We also become "good" at it. When we "don't act like ourselves" we are probably using the weaker auxiliary, tertiary or the weakest of all the preferences which is called the inferior or shadow, or a combination of our weak preferences which we usually do not like to use.

The concept of "preferences" or "human talents" has essentially the same meaning as "charisms." Some people refer to their human talents as natural gifts. Others refer to those same human talents as gifts from God. Therefore, and hereafter in this book we will use the concepts of talents, preferences, functions and charisms interchangeably.

> From the reception of these charisms or gifts, including those which are less dramatic, there arises for each believer the right and duty to use them in the Church and the world for the good of humankind and for the upbuilding of the Church.[2]

Charisms in the Old and New Testaments are personal talents freely given by God and developed by individuals in the productive service of fulfilling the needs of others in the parish community. In this context, St. Paul uses the personal charisms of individuals to help structure the community (1 Cor. 12: 7; Rom. 12: 4; Eph. 4:7). The Church is the Body of Christ with many diverse members, each member having his/her own special charisms. The Church is built on the foundation of the many diverse charisms of deacons, kings, prophets, doctors, martyrs, apostles and disciples: all persons.

Leaders must never stifle, but rather cooperate with the Holy Spirit in encouraging and empowering persons to exercise their charisms in service to others (1 Thes. 5:19). Leaders must realize that *all* charisms are important and useful, and must be allowed to function appropriately in the Church. Each charism, when released in service for the common good, makes its own beautiful, different and complementary contribution to building God's kingdom here on earth. However, according to Boff

> . . . the constant temptation in the Church is that of having power over others, of one charism prevailing over other charisms to the point of silencing them. The Church then runs the risk . . . of being a community that only hears dogmas, rites, canonical prescriptions, edifying exhortations, and not the liberating word of God.[3]

The Charisms of Introversion (I) and Extraversion (E)

The word "energy" can help us understand our preference for either introversion or extraversion. Persons who are introverts prefer to use their energy in quiet ways, alone or with a friend or two. Introverts are actually energized in these quiet activities. Their energy is sapped when they are involved in several meetings or social events which require them to be with a lot of people and a variety of people. They are energized by quiet and reflection. They are de-energized by the opposite.

Since extraverts are the opposites of introverts, they are energized by a lot of activity, the more people the merrier. Parties, meetings and social activities of all kinds are important to them and actually needed in order to retain their energy for life. Without people, they are de-energized.

The "ideal" balance between introversion and extraversion is to have a clear-cut preference for one over the other while retaining the capacity to use the lesser-preferred function when needed. The two, with one being clearly stronger, provides balance for the person. The person who is "extremely" introverted can be reclusive. The person who is "extremely" extraverted can be an irresponsible gadfly. (In Appendix A, list the names of the I's and E's who are on your parish leadership team.)

When a person does not exhibit a clear-cut preference for either introversion or extraversion, this person will transmit mixed messages to friends, family members and co-workers. If, at times, this person turns to people and gives the impression that he/she enjoys their constant companionship and interaction . . . . and then, at times (too often) turns inward and avoids the same people without sufficient explanation, confusion results. Uneven introversion/extraversion behavior indicates that the two preferences are too closely balanced. Theory and practice indicate that one preference should be the dominant one. The other preference is an auxiliary preference ready and waiting to assist the person to adapt to the world and the people in it, and to the important inner world of self. To live in both worlds is to live with balance, happiness and effectiveness.

The Charisms of iNtuition (N) and Sensing (S)

Intuition and sensing are two mental functions that help persons gather information. Sensing people use their five senses to see, hear, touch, taste and smell what is actually happening here and now. They tend to be practical and realistic because they believe that their senses would not lie to them. The information received from their senses are facts and realities which make them sensible and realistic persons. They deal with what is actually happening and what has happened. To speculate about what could be is a waste of precious present time which must be used to live in the present.

While sensing persons are concrete and practical, intuitive persons are creative and innovative. Sensing persons live in the present. Intuitives live in the future. Sensing persons tend to be accurate in their work, like details and look for the literal meaning of things. The intuitives dislike doing what the sensing persons enjoy doing or what comes easily to the sensing person. Instead the intuitives like to focus on the big picture; they scan and glance at people, things and written articles; they enjoy imagery and the metaphor. The sensing persons do their learning in a linear, step-by-step process. The intuitives use the opposite approach. They are global learners who see the whole picture by way of hunch or intuition, and without understanding how they know. They become accustomed to listening to that inner voice helping them to understand complex ideas "instantly." The intuitives are likely to say, "Oh yes, it just came to me!" The intuitives do not understand how they could understand something so quickly; and, the sensing persons distrust their instantaneous knowledge because "they did not work it out step-by-step."

Of the four sets of preferences, sensing/intuition causes the most misunderstanding, distrust, miscommunication and grief between persons who prefer sensing and those who prefer intuition. One of the goals of this book is to help people of opposite personality-types try to understand and appreciate other people for what they are. Persons in today's world must be extremely interdependent. Consequently, sensing people must rely on their own strengths, realize the weaknesses of their own type, and depend on the intuitives to complement them with their vision, the big picture, a look into the future, creativity and innovation. At the same time, intuitives must depend upon the sensing persons for their practical and realistic approach to life. They have the facts and they can focus on what is happening. When these two personality types strain to work together, they can enjoy the best of all worlds: the past, present and future.

Individual persons must make an effort to balance their lives by using both functions, with one function being the more preferred, stronger and more dependable preference. This is the dominant function. The other is the auxiliary function which allows for flexibility and balance. Therefore, the healthy personality-type is the person who is able to use sensing and intuition when needed.

Whereas the sensing person views the intuitive as "spacy," flighty and impractical, the intuitive sees the sensing person mired in details; unchanging and unimaginative. With proper balance, a person can live in the real world and be aware that future vision is needed also. Uneven social behavior indicates that the two preferences are too closely meshed. Theory and practice indicate that one preference should be the dominant one, and the other preference an auxiliary function, ready and waiting to assist the person to adapt to the world and the people in it and to the important inner world of self. To live in both worlds is to live with balance, happiness and effectiveness.

Both charisms, sensing and intuition, are needed in the parish and in the Church. We must always be reminded about the joys and realities of the present and past while being aware that hope is eternal.

(In Appendix A, list the names of the people on your parish leadership team who are S's and N's.)

The Charisms of Thinking (T) and Feeling (F)

Everyone makes decisions in their lives. Some people prefer to make decisions based on an objective and logical decision-making process. These are the people who prefer to think through the process before making their decisions. Other people prefer to make decisions based on a personal and value-laden process. These are the people who depend on their feelings to lead them to their decisions. Each is a valid and rational way toward decision-making. However, as with the other functions, people prefer one or the other and are good at using their preference.

People who prefer to use the thinking function possess skills of analysis, synthesis, objective evaluation. Their attitude is one of impartiality, fairness and justice. This impersonal basis of choice helps them to use their thinking skills in difficult situations which call for toughmindedness and the ability to take a firm stand.

People who prefer to use the feeling function can be good decision makers as well. However, they make their decisions on a personal basis which the thinking people have difficulty in understanding. Feeling people need to be appreciated. They seek harmony in their relationships. Feeling people try to convince people by persuasion and on sympathetic feelings for humanity. Whereas, thinking people try to convince people by logical argumentation based on laws and principles.

The healthy personality type is balanced: utilizing thinking skills and expressing humane feelings and values. By contrast, without this balance, a person can become either a hard-hearted monster or an emotional cripple. It is important, however, that a person have a clear-cut preference for one or the other. The dominant preference provides an individual with a powerful and consistent process for making decisions. The weaker and less used auxiliary function is always there to provide the flexibility in the decision making process.

At times throughout history, the Church seemed to be too much of a "thinking" Church, i.e., a theological "head" Church without much emotion or feeling. The Church must appeal to all persons, including feeling and thinking persons. And, persons must be encouraged to use their charism of feeling as well as their charism of thinking.

The charisms of logic and thinking best serve the Church when they are balanced with the charisms of feeling, i.e., the things of the heart.

(In Appendix A, list the names of the people on your parish leadership team who are T's and F's.)

The Charisms of Judging (J) and Perceiving (P)

A fourth set of charisms are judging and perceiving. Judging people enjoy making decisions, coming to conclusions and closure. They have a strong work ethic which leads them to be productive. Their life-style depends on planning ahead, settling things quickly, being decisive, meeting deadlines, honoring commitments, living in an orderly, routinized and fixed way.

The life-style of perceiving persons could drive the judging people "up a wall." They are free-wheeling, go-with-the-flow people who enjoy life and have more of a play ethic. They like to be flexible and prefer to leave situations open-ended, so that they may have more time to reflect, perceive and discern life and the happenings of life. They tend to be process oriented, not in a hurry to make decisions. They prefer to wait and see what will happen.

Both of these preferences are needed to give proper balance to one's life. People need to perceive and discern before they make decisions. However, it is necessary to do both. Without the quality of perceiving, a person could easily be a dictator. Without the quality of judging, a person could be labeled a "flake." A person who possesses both preferences in a balanced way could prove to be a perceptive decision maker.

Leaders must encourage and empower persons to use their charism of judging in order to assure justice in the world. At the same time, the charism of perception is needed to assure flexibility for a Church in a changing world.

It must be repeated here once again how important it is to have one strong and dominant preference so that persons can rely confidently, comfortably and consistently on their strong suit. The other preference supports and complements and allows for flexibility when a person is faced with making a decision.

It should be clear from the above descriptions how important the charisms of judging and perceiving are for the Church. Either one without the other would bring disastrous results to the Church. It goes without saying that the existence and use of all of the above charisms are essentially crucial to any institution, including the institution of the Church.

(In Appendix A, list the names of the people on your parish leadership team who are J's or P's.)

> Indeed, everyone should painstakingly ready himself or herself personally for the apostolate, especially as an adult. For the advance of age brings with it better self-knowledge, thus enabling each person to evaluate more accurately the talents with which God has enriched each soul and to exercise more effectively those charismatic gifts which the Holy Spirit has bestowed on all for the good of others.[4]

The Four Basic Personality-Types

Every healthy institution requires teamwork from its employees and employers, leaders and followers. No institution could survive if all of its people were salespersons; or if they were all public relations people; or if they were all accountants. Every healthy institution needs a nice mix of people who possess different skills, attitudes and competencies. Good teamwork requires valuable complementary differences and strengths among members of a team.

> When the two functions of Sensing and Intuition are combined with the Thinking and Feeling functions, four basic combinations result: Sensing plus Thinking (ST); Sensing plus Feeling (SF); Intuition plus Feeling (NF); Intuition plus Thinking (NT). Each combination produces a stronger set of charisms, values, leadership styles, and a unique sense of vision.

> *Sensing plus Thinking:* The ST people are mainly interested in facts, since facts are what can be collected and verified directly by the senses, by seeing, hearing, touching, etc. And they make decisions on these facts by impersonal analysis, because

what they trust is thinking, with its step-by-step process of reasoning from cause to effect, from premise to conclusion.

Sensing plus Feeling: The SF people are also interested in facts, but make their decisions with personal warmth, because what they trust is feeling, with its power to weigh how much things matter to themselves and others.

Intuition plus Feeling: The NF people judge with the same personal warmth. But since they prefer intuition, their interest is not in facts but in possibilities, such as new projects, things that have not happened but might be made to happen, or new truths that are not yet known but might be found out.

Intuition plus Thinking: The NT people share the interest in possibilities. But since they prefer thinking, they approach these with impersonal analysis. Often the possibility they choose is a theoretical, technical or executive one, with the human element more or less ignored.[5]

Leaders can make people feel noble, honorable and worthwhile when they recognize and acknowledge their special charisms, and when they empower people to use their charisms for the common good. This is an ennobling process. Just as God the Creator created man and woman to be noble creatures by breathing a spiritual soul into an animal body, parishes can transform people by ennobling and empowering them.

The beautiful differences and varied strengths of the many people who work in the Church can help the Church be more caring, more knowing, more responsible and more respectful. What is needed is for leaders of the Church to understand that people do indeed have different interests, strengths, weaknesses, values and needs. Leaders with this kind of understanding will rely on the person with an intuitive charism for a clear vision of the future; on the person with a sensing charism for concrete realism; on the person with a thinking charism for logical analysis; on the person with a feeling charism for dealing with people.

The effective leader will help lessen friction in the parish or diocese by getting opposite types to complement one another in a team leadership approach. Synergistic teamwork will produce a healthy parish and diocese.

As persons feel more noble and worthwhile, so too will the parish and diocese. The Church will be viewed as an effective leader.

The Church As a Corporate Personality-Type

When we view the institution of the Church as a corporate person, each parish has a personality-type. This is so because the leaders of the parish can produce a shared parish vision and philosophy, specific parish values, preferred behaviors in serving parishioners, a prioritized set of needs, and specific goals and objectives to help the parish fulfill its unique mission.

The actions of any institution often seem randomly varied. In reality, they follow patterns. Just as Jung said that a person's behavior actually follows patterns and these patterns are called psychological types, it is our notion that institutional behavior follows the patterns of corporate psychological-types.

As a corporate person, the Church takes on a variety of psychological types depending on its leadership at any given period of history. Church leaders actually follow the patterns of their psychological types. Believers in the Church spontaneously adhere to a particular model of Church. Avery Dulles, in his book *Models of Church*, evaluates his five models of Church and concludes that:

> certain types of persons will be spontaneously drawn to certain models. Church officials have a tendency to prefer the institutional model; ecumenists, the community model; speculative theologians, the sacramental model; preachers and biblical scholars, the kerygmatic model; and secular activists, the servant model.[6]

Dulles' basic idea of typological approach resulted from H.R. Niebuhr's book, *Christ and Culture,* in which Niebuhr writes about five types of visions of the relationship between Christ and human culture. We agree with Dulles when he says that typology can have great value in helping people to get beyond the limitations of their own particular outlook, and to enter into fruitful conversation with others having a fundamentally different mentality.[7]

5

A Unique Spirit Animates Parishes

Members of the Academie Internationale d'Heraldique are skilled heraldic artisans who design Coats of Arms for bishops of the Church. A Coat of Arms contains a "blazon" and a "motto." The symbolism of each could represent family heritage and an individual's values. The symbolism on a bishop's Coat of Arms can reveal many significant hidden meanings about basic values that are most important to him; that he focuses on and most identifies with; that he is proud to be noted for and willing to instill in his followers. The motto on a bishop's Coat of Arms encapsulates his most basic values as they relate to the institution of the Church. His values and how he communicates them will attract people to the Church, or turn people away from it.

If American presidents had Coats of Arms, the motto on President Bush's heraldic shield might be "A Kinder and Gentler Nation." Other presidents focused on particular values. Their mottos might have been: "Carry A Big Stick" (Theodore Roosevelt); "We Must Restore The Torn Fabric Of Our Common Life" (Franklin D. Roosevelt); "Give 'em Hell" (Harry Truman); "Unity . . . Let's Do It My Way" (Lyndon B. Johnson); "Ask What You Can Do For Your Country" (John F. Kennedy).

As President Bush began his presidency he focused on being more kind to the homeless by investigating ways to solve this horrible social problem. He stressed the importance of making the United States a gentler nation by focusing on ways to solve the terrible dilemma of chemical addiction and its debilitating effects on the country. His values were clearly stated. It remains to be seen how he animates his followers with his values. President Truman was a forthright, plain speaking leader. He did not mince words about how he felt on issues and about people. Some believe that his decision to drop atom bombs on the people of Japan emanated from his no-nonsense, prioritized set of values. The preferred values of each president have precipitated specific decisions and certain actions.

Church leaders also reveal plenty about themselves when they publicly affirm their preferred values. By stating their values they give us insights about how they view the traditional Church; how they envision the future Church; how they plan to use the power that has been given to them; how they intend to work with people; what they intend to achieve; what their priorities are, etc. The motto on a bishop's Coat of Arms gives us an initial clue about his primary values. I have compiled a random sampling of a number of mottos, and the bishop's name and diocese.[1]

"Semper Idem" (Always the Same) was a famous motto. It was adopted by Cardinal Ottavianni several years before Vatican II was planned or even thought about. Would you believe that he was the chief protagonist and foremost opponent of Vatican II, and bitterly fought against any changes proposed by the Council?

Another famous motto is that of Cardinal Krol: "Deus Rex Deus." Can we deduce from his motto what values he espoused? Did his leadership flow from his basic values? What type of Church is valued based on this motto?

Diocese	Bishop	Motto
Albany	Hubbard	Rejoice! We Are His People
Arlington	Keating	Be Rooted In Him
Belleville	Keleher	One Body One Spirit
Biloxi	Howze	Unity of God's People
Brooklyn	Mulrooney	Love One Another
Cincinnati	Pilarczyk	Bonitas Justitia Veritas
Covington	Hughes	To Serve Not To Be Served
Denver	Stafford	In The Beginning The Word
Des Moines	Bullock	Grace Mercy Peace
Detroit	Szoka	To Live In Faith

Dodge City	Schlarman	Who Is A Rock But Our God
Erie	Murphy	Pax et Misericordia
Fairbanks	Kaniecki	To Love and To Serve
Fargo	Sullivan	Lord Teach Us
Fresno	Madera	To Jesus Through Mary
Gallup	Hastrich	Ut Omnes Unum Sumus
Gary	Gaughan	Grant A Heart That Listens
Green Bay	Maida	Facere Omnia Nova
Hartford	Whealon	Vox Clamantis In Deserto
Helena	Curtiss	That We May All Be One
Honolulu	Ferrario	My Grace Is All You Need
Lake Charles	Speyrer	To Bring Glad Tidings
Lexington	William	Act Justly, Love Tenderly
Los Angeles	Mahony	To Reconcile God's People
Military Services USA	Ryan	Pro Pace In Terris
Milwaukee	Weakland	Aequalis Omnibus Caritas
New York	O'Connor	There Can Be No Love Without Justice
Norwich	Reilly	In Kindness and In Truth
Paterson	Rodimer	Maranatha
Peoria	O'Rourke	To Lead By Serving
Phoenix	O'Brien	To Build Up The Body of Christ
Pittsburgh	Wuerl	Thy Kingdom Come
Sante Fe	Sanchez	Instrumentum Pacis
Santa Rosa	Steinbock	All For The Love Of God
Parma (Byz)	Pataki	Hear Me O Lord
Caroline-Marshall Islands	Samo	The Islands Put Their Hope in the Lord

What is the significance of the above mottos? It means that a variety of personality-types who happen to be bishops have different preferences, just like the rest of us. They focus on and emphasize different values. When working with one another in the National Conference of Catholic Bishops (NCCB), their values can become conflicting or complementary values.

As heads of dioceses, their values can animate people with a sense of identity, pride and purpose. Their shared and complementary values can give life, form and vitality to their dioceses and to their parishes.

When leaders are able to clarify their own values and publicly affirm those values as important standards by which they live and work, their lives become more purposeful. They know what they want. They feel more positive about themselves. They have a cause to work for. They feel "value-able."

Effective leaders are enthusiastic about sharing their deep-seated values with others. They are enspirited (people with values) who can attract followers and animate their lives and their work with a similar sense of purpose. They move people. They have a sense of identity because "who they are" and "how they live" rises from what they believe in. They have a sense of pride because they are happy and proud to be known as people with values and purpose.

Case studies presented in the books *Theory Z, Principles of Japanese Management* and *Pursuit of Excellence* clearly indicate that effective leaders are the ones who are "singleminded" in purpose. That is, they know what they want, what is important to them and do everything they can to achieve that valued purpose.

When leaders enspirit others, they help people become more productive. Enspiriting-leaders create conditions, based on their values, that give people a sense of accomplishment and productivity. To be productive is very gratifying. To be productive is itself a value and when people feel productive they have a sense of personal worth and pride.

When leaders enspirit others, they build a team spirit based on mutual respect for each other's values and person. Leaders can count on people who know what they want, who believe strongly in something, and follow up on their commitments and values. When the inevitable conflicts arise, the leadership team that has members who respect the values of other team members have a better chance of resolving their conflicts.

There are many wonderful examples throughout our world's history of singleminded people who publicly affirmed their basic values and were able to attract hundreds, thousands and even millions of followers. Their special "Spirit" gave life, form and vitality to a specific type of "institution."

Francis of Assisi valued poverty and humility and these values (his special type of Spirit) have given life, form and vitality to Franciscan communities throughout the world. St. Benedict's "Spirit" of prayer and work (Ora et Labora) gave life, form and vitality to monasticism. Jean Baptiste de LaSalle and Mother Elizabeth Seton were enspirited with a love for Catholic schools and gave life, form and vitality to great Catholic schools throughout the world. The founding fathers of the United States of America cherished the values of independence, freedom and equality, and gave life, form and vitality to a new nation.

Members of each of the above "institutions" have the responsibility to nourish, maintain and enhance the Spirit of their founders. At times, Spirit must be renewed or re-formed in order to give new life, form and vitality to old institutions. Each member of the institution should exhibit a distinctive identity, pride and purpose in being a Franciscan, Benedictine, Christian Brother, Sister of Charity, and an American. We talk, at times, about "school spirit" and "team spirit."

Philip Selznick wrote beautifully about the importance of values in his book, *Leadership and Administration:*

> The formation of an institution is marked by the making of value commitments, that is, choices which fix the assumptions of policy makers as to the nature of the enterprise, its distinctive aims, methods, and roles .... The institutional leader is primarily an expert in the promotion and protection of values .... Leadership fails when it concentrates on sheer survival. Institutional survival, properly understood, is a matter of maintaining values and distinctive identity.[2]

IBM's Thomas Watson, Jr. corroborates and adds to Selznick's remarks when he says:

> Consider any great organization—one that has lasted over the years—I think you will find that it owes its resiliency not to its

form of organization or administrative skills, but to the power of what we call beliefs and the appeal these beliefs have for its people. This then is my thesis: I firmly believe that any organization, in order to survive and achieve success, must have a sound set of beliefs on which it premises all its policies and actions. Next, I believe that the most important single factor in corporate success is faithful adherence to those beliefs. And, finally, I believe if an organization is to meet the challenge of a changing world, it must be prepared to change everything about itself except those beliefs . . . . the basic philosophy, spirit, and drive of an organization have far more to do with its relative achievements than do technological or economic resources, organizational structure, innovation, and timing.[3]

All effective and successful leaders possess a Spirit that attracts individuals to join them in their institutions. Leaders appeal to their interests, values and purposes in life. It is our belief that followers are attracted spontaneously to any person or institution that espouses their preferred values and incorporates them in the life-style of the institution. When leaders interiorize and actually live out the values they profess, and when they provide real opportunities for their followers to do the same, an electric climate is created of which people want to be a part. An enspiriting process has begun: individuals begin to acquire a sense of identity, a sense of pride, a sense of shared values which bond them together, a sense of purpose which gives them hope and perseverance, and a sense of vitality which offers freshness and continued life. The enspiriting process creates a special force that animates persons. We call this force SPIRIT and we define it in the following way.

> *SPIRIT is an energizing force, arising from one's values, that animates individuals with a sense of identity, pride, and purpose; and, it gives life, specific form and vitality to institutions.*

In the institution of the Church, baptism actually begins the enspiriting process. Baptism initiates us into the community of the Church. The reception of the sacraments and active participation in the life of the Church strengthens our Church membership. There should be a distinctive pride in being a Catholic. Church leaders have the responsibility to help its members "forge an identity with the Church that can be carried easily and with poise in his or her life . . . ."[4]

Companies which have been judged to be excellent also believe in a set of values, and believe firmly that their shared values actually bond their workers.

> Texas Instruments, Procter & Gamble, 3M and IBM, for example, all pay close attention to the customer and each has a highly developed value system that causes its employees to identify strongly with the firm. Perhaps the intense loyalty that these firms inspire is just an interesting idiosyncrasy. But we believe, on the contrary, that this bond of shared values is fundamental to all of the rest. In our view, this is probably the most underpublicized 'secret weapon' of great companies.[5]

Church leaders should do all that is possible to bond each person to the Church by reaching out to people everywhere, inviting them to live as holy people in one community which has a rich past, a loving and caring present, and a stable institution which offers continuity and hope for the future. When people interiorize the values of the Church, a sense of purpose grows in its members. This animating spirit creates bonds among Church members, and gives vitality and life to the Church as a human institution. When people are energized by this spirit, they have pride, an esprit-de-corps, a sense of identity, and a willingness to serve their brothers and sisters as a Church, as a parish community. They are animated with the "spirit-ual" energy to uplift others in the Church and in the parish.

This is a Church whose spirit is "type-ified" as One, Holy, Catholic and Apostolic. In other words, this special spirit flows directly and spontaneously from one's basic innately and environmentally shaped personality-type. It influences individual persons in their preference for a style of Christianity and a "type" of Church.

Spirit is both means and end. As a means toward an end, it can be understood as a prevailing climate or mood which keeps people excited and enthusiastic about what they are doing. It can be compared to the electric excitement that energizes actors and actresses immediately preceding the opening of their Broadway musical; the same spirit that remains with them during the actual performance. The adrenelin flows. The performers are "psyched-up." This kind of spirit uplifts them as a means toward a successful theatrical production.

Spirit is an end also. It is something to be attained, a final state, a workplace, an environment, an institution where it is good to be. When people do not have a good spirit, it is something to be worked for. It becomes a final product.

Spirit can typify a Church that is One; a type of Church that is Holy; a type of Church that is Catholic; a type of Church that is Apostolic. These are the four characteristic "marks" of the Church. Each one marks the Church with a special and specific type of spirit. Each type of spirit which flows spontaneously from its own personality-type gives its own special nuance to the Church. Consequently, the Church must be adaptable to the marvelous variety of persons. She must incorporate all within Herself.

According to the methodology of this book, there are four types of SPIRIT that animate persons and parishes.

1. *Parishes and persons who have an **Apostolic Spirit** value the basic need to remain in visible apostolic continuity with the church's own origins and to be in conformity with the institution of christ.*

The institution of the Church has a beautiful heritage and meaningful traditions. Important to them is the idea of an institutional Church which makes sure that there is a tomorrow. This past, present and future focus provides a force for stability and continuity which binds people together into a Church which is apostolic. Parishes and parishioners who are filled with these basic values and this type of philosophy try to attract, engage, bond and uplift followers with this unique spirit. The parish bonds their parishioners with a special identity. They identify with the heritage and traditions of the Church. They are proud of the Church's past. It is their renewed purpose to continue this past tradition into the future. It is this spirit of apostolicity that will help sustain the life, form and vitality of their parish as they view it.

Church leaders and the faithful who are influenced by this spirit of authenticity value the Church primarily as a Church that is in visible continuity with its own apostolic origins. They believe strongly that Church members must focus on the essential teachings of the Church, and that they are in absolute conformity with the will of Christ and with the institution of the Church. It is only through this continuity of apostolic authority that the Church can carry on Christ's work in its pastoral ministry, in its sacramental ministry, and in the sanctifying work of Christ himself. It is Christ himself who has commanded his apostles and their successors to carry out His work.

An apostolic spirit in the Church is characterized by a stability which is caused by a strong attachment to all of the beautiful and wonderful memories of the past. What this type of leader and follower must realize, however, is how the Church has changed in relation to the evolving patterns of human culture. In addition, they must realize that our present institution of the Church and its current organizational forms have changed and evolved through a complex variety of political, social, ecclesial, cultural, and philosophical happenings throughout history's course. Church leaders and followers must remain faithful to everything that is authentic in the Church. At the same time, they must be flexible enough to carry out the mission of Christ in organized structures that fit the cultural times.

> 2. *Parishes and persons who have a* **Catholic Spirit** *value the basic need to reach out to people everywhere and to serve them by fulfilling their highest priority needs.*

Mutual service among people of every nation binds them together into a Church which is catholic, i.e., universal. People in parishes who possess a spirit of catholicity are willing to reach out to parishioners of neighboring parishes and in surrounding communities for the purpose of serving their needs in addition to their own. This type of Church and its leaders are filled with these basic values and this type of serving philosophy. They try to attract, engage, bond and uplift others with this unique spirit. They animate their followers with a special sense of serving people. Service to people everywhere provides for them a sense of identity, pride and purpose. The spirit of catholicity is a force that helps people sustain a life of serving others. By serving others they are animated and energized.

The Church is universal. Christ redeemed the entire human race through his life, death and resurrection. And the Church continues Christ's universal redemptive work and expresses it in the service of fulfilling human needs. This service reaches out to everyone, everywhere, and it includes the elderly, children, men and women of every condition and of every race, saints and sinners, rich and poor, everyone. Since Christ died for all, the Church must be alive for all.

> . . . if I washed your feet—I who am Teacher and Lord—then you must wash each other's feet. What I just did was to give you an example: as I have done, so you must do (John 13: 13-15).

Serving is a sign of Christ's caring presence and a response to the needs of people everywhere. Serving people causes people to be transformed in hope and happiness. Christians in a serving Catholic Church and local parish become living signs of love in the world by feeding its hungry, providing homes for the many homeless, giving clothes to those who cannot afford them, caring for the sick, teaching, and offering any service that brings dignity to individuals, and justice and peace in the world.

The spirit of reaching out to everyone everywhere and serving them is a means towards fulfilling the Church's objective of service and Christ's mandate for charity. The Church has a moral obligation to all of Christ's redeemed people.

This means that the Church must be Indian to the Indian, Hispanic to the Hispanic, Black to the Black, White to the White, Korean to the Korean, Feminine to the Feminine, Male to the Male, Adult to the Adult . . . . It must be all things to all people. The unchangeable message of Christ must be continually adjusted to the diversity and variety of human factors in our mosaic world. Existing side by side throughout history is the principle of stability and the principle of change.

The Church of Christ must reach out in actual fact to the whole world as Bishop Maximos IV indicates:

We must be convinced that Christianity can never accomplish its mission in the world unless it is catholic; that is, universal, not only in principle but also in actual fact. If one cannot be Catholic unless he gives up his own liturgy, hierarchy, patristic traditions, history, hymnography, art, language, culture, and spiritual heritage, and adopts the rites, philosophical and theological thought, religious poetry, liturgical language, culture, and spirituality of a particular group, be it the best, then the Church is not a great gift of God to the whole world but a faction, however numerous, and a human institution subservient to the interests of one group. Such a Church could not be the true Church of Christ.[6]

Bishop Maximos challenges us to recognize the other beautiful types of spirit which animate people in diverse effective ways and in their diverse and beautiful cultures. By stretching ourselves beyond the limits of our personality-types and our own particular traditions we become more complete and whole human beings. And, our Church and parish is enriched. They become healthier and, in fact, universal.

Bishop Maximos is challenging the Church to be universal, in fact. Parishes and parishioners are being asked daily to come face to face with other "thoughtforms." This could result in new explanations and new structures. In fact, in the United States, in Europe, in Latin American countries, and in all Third World countries, the Church is facing on-going challenges to respect the thoughtforms of new cultures, new thinking, new times, new languages, new socioeconomics, new bioethical situations, new environmental and global forces. The Church is being challenged every day to fill the world with its universal spirit of reaching out. It must reach out with its authentic, unchangeable message of Jesus Christ and adjust it in fundamentally new ways.

> 3. *Parishes and persons, who have a* **Spirit of Wanting To Be One,** *value the basic need to live together as brothers and sisters in one community of faith, trust and mutual concern.*

This spirit of oneness creates an esprit-de-corps which binds people together into a parish which is unified. This type of parish and its leaders are filled with these basic values and a specific type of philosophy. They try to attract, engage, bond and uplift followers with this unique spirit. The spirit of oneness animates individuals by drawing them together to form personal relationships and a sense of community. To form a community gives them a purpose. To be a part of a community gives them a special identity and a sense of pride. Unity is the primary form of the parish. Striving for a continued sense of parish community provides parishioners with vitality and energy.

The Church is and must be one. People who love the idea of community prefer to focus on this type of Church and parish. Forming a parish community and living with this type of spirit energizes people as they try to treat one another with mutual trust and concern. They live in fellowship and in unity, or are striving for it.

> I give you a new commandment: Love one another. Such as
> my love has been for you, so must your love be for each other.
> This is how all will know you for my disciples: your love for
> one another (John 13: 34-35).

The Church is One when its members are united to one another in mutual love, when they worship together, when their behavior gives evidence that they are brothers and sisters in the One Lord. Healthy personal relationships grow into Christian friendship and fellowship, and into a community gathered around its unifying force: Jesus Christ.

People who value the idea of unity come together as a Church of responding persons. And they come together in the Lord's name. The skills, talents and charisms of individual persons are discerned and recognized, and they are blended together to form one strong group. Meeting in faith they give hope to each other. Their one-ness is an expression of their love for God and for one another.

A personal relationship with Christ and personal relationships with one another are their values. They are the keys to being one in mind, heart and action. Bonds of friendship are formed; a collaborative spirit prevails; mutual trust builds; a new sense of interdependence helps unite individuals. A common value system is accepted and it replaces individualistic life-styles. An active spirituality characterizes the group's inner feeling for each other.

Sharing a common value system and living out the traditions and customs of the community help individuals fulfill their own unique sense of individuality. When effective community-leaders are able to reinforce the importance of their shared values by word and example, it becomes more probable that followers will actually live out those values in more conscientious ways.

4. *Parishes and persons, who have a* **Spirit of Holiness,** *value the basic need to live holy and distinguished lives, and work toward establishing an institution of holiness and distinction.*

Their values are usually contrary to the popular values expressed in contemporary worldly culture and in a contemporary institution which might be adversely affected by the corruption of the world. Their values can be counter-cultural. This type of Church and its leaders are filled with the basic values and philosophy of challenge, change, reform, distinction and excellence. They try to attract, engage, bond and uplift others with their unique spirit. The spirit of holiness is a force for change, renewal and revitalization. This force animates people to be a part of an evolving, ever-changing institution. Its vitality is rooted in the willingness of its members to scrutinize themselves and their parish, and to muster up the courage to seek holiness and excellence.

The Church is an institution of holiness. Members of a parish who focus on this characteristic value have the primary belief that the Church institution and its members must undergo constant reform and conversion to the gospel. The institution of the Church must purify itself of its faults. The leaders and followers must purify themselves of their faults. The task of personal and organizational reform and renewal must always be pursued so that the Church will remain true to its vocation of holiness: its ability to remain in the world but not of it. By being holy, the Church stands against the world as a "sign of contradiction." It is in the world but distinct from it.

Christ loved the Church and delivered himself up for it, that he might sanctify it . . . that he might present to himself a glorious

Church, not having spot or wrinkle . . . but holy and without
blemish (Eph. 5: 25-28).

The Church is holy in its mission and its purpose which is the same as
Christ's: to redeem us from sin and to make us one with Him. Belloso
describes the sanctity of Jesus as a harmonic whole which includes dissonant notes. For instance, the gospel of St. Mark begins with Jesus teaching. And then, there are five scenes (Mark 2: 30-36) describing Jesus disconcerting his followers:

1) Jesus forgives the sins of the paralytic;

2) Jesus eats with sinners;

3) Jesus gives approval to people who do not fast while indicating that
   only new wine should be poured in new wineskins;

4) Jesus attests to his authority and dominion over the Sabbath;

5) Jesus breaks the Sabbath when he cures a man with a withered hand.

Jesus seems to be disobeying the Judaic laws, laws purported to make
men and women holy when they are followed rigorously. Jesus refuses to
carry out some man-made law simply to please God. Actually, Jesus is
presenting himself as the means of grace and salvation. His words and actions are distinct from and transcend the law. The holiness of Jesus not
only shocks people, it empowers sinful and lowly men and women to raise
themselves up: the sinner, the embarrassed wedding hosts, the man with
the withered hand, people enslaved by the law, etc.

The positive characteristics of the holiness of Jesus can be expressed in
"I am" type phrases found in the gospel of St. John:

I am forgiveness; I am the center of the community of sinners;
I am the bridegroom; I am the Lord of the Sabbath; I am salvation and life. This makes it possible to speak of the arrival of
the holiness of God himself in the midst of humanity. And it
makes Jesus, rather than someone trying to carry out the law to
the letter or establish religious observance as a supreme value,
the man who in his person, words and actions, shows and expresses the gratuitous and saving love of God for those lacking

fulness in their lives. This . . . characterizes the holiness of Jesus.[7]

When the Church, as a human institution, is lacking fulness in itself it must "shock" itself with necessary renewal. It does this by empowering people to raise themselves up. The People of God are asked to respond to God's invitation to holiness by the Church:

> Thus it is evident to everyone that all the faithful of Christ of whatever rank or status are called to the fulness of the Christian life and to the perfection of charity. By this holiness a more human way of life is promoted even in this earthly society.[8]

In conclusion to this chapter, parishes use an enspiriting process when they are able to attract others to the values which they hold in high esteem, and bond those people together. Their lives are uplifted because values give their lives new meaning and a distinct purpose. This entire process gives rise and form to a holy and distinguished parish which has the capacity to transform the lives of its members. This type of institution can be a powerhouse for society because it is One, Holy, Catholic and Apostolic.

> An institution is a gathering of persons who have accepted a common purpose, and a common discipline to guide the pursuit of that purpose, to the end that each involved person reaches higher fulfillment as a person, through serving and being served by the common venture, than would be achieved alone or in a less committed relationship.[9]

6

A Shared Vision Guides Parishes

> We do not look from the present into the future, but from the future into the present.[1]

For a leader (a parish, a diocese or a person) to have vision and share it is to paint a dream. It is a mental image of what is possible and desirable. Some call it foresight, or the ability to see around corners.

Followers prefer a leader who believes wholeheartedly in something, who stands for something, who shares personal values and who shares a vision. The leader enables followers to help make realities out of dreams. The leader's vision engulfs people and seems to pull them toward the vision. People gain confidence in the leader and in themselves because they feel important, wanted, useful and needed. They feel that they are necessary components in fulfilling that dream. When leaders convince their followers that the vision is extremely important and difficult to achieve, and when leaders give a clear picture of the vision, preconditions for success are established and followers are energized to work toward a common end.

In their book, *Leaders*, Bennis and Nanus draw four specific conclusions from 60 interviews with successful CEO's from prestigious companies and 30 interviews with top leaders in the arts, sports and government. The most significant finding was that all 90 leaders were "vision-oriented."

In effect, successful and effective leaders are visionaries, persons who clearly communicate a blueprint for the future. It is a blueprint which focuses on "doing the right thing" rather than on "doing things right." By focusing their attention on a vision they enable people emotionally and spiritually to fulfill that dream. They have a clear vision of the direction their institution should go, clearly communicate the vision, receive commitment from persons in the institution, and are able to accomplish the intended results.

> Leaders are people whose focus always is on results. Through a hard-to-define, perhaps even mystical blending of inspiration, imagination and initiative, they formulate a vision of the future, their own future, and the organization's future. And they are able to transmit their values and their vision to their associates. This permits a harmonious team to accomplish far more than the same number of people could accomplish working alone, or in an authoritarian group.[2]

Spirit and Vision go hand-in-hand. The values of "one, holy, catholic and apostolic" provide an animating spirit. Fundamental values encapsulate in brief and understandable words why the institution exists, what its mission is, what its tradition and culture are all about. When people share common values, an atmosphere is created in which people are seen as "value-able." They have significant value.

Expecting the unexpected, knowing the unknowable, and accepting change in a rapidly changing world must all be considered as a way of life for any leader, including the parish. We need leaders who can roll with the punches and handle the unexpected events of life. We need leaders who see challenges instead of obstacles, and opportunities instead of problems. What remains hidden to most must be visible to the leader who is creative enough to build better and more caring institutions in the world. When a leader empowers others with a unique spirit and a challenging vision, and invites them to be co-equal on a team of equals, dreams can become realities.

> Leadership is the process of persuasion and example by which an individual or leadership team induces a group to take action that is in accord with the leader's purposes or, most likely, the shared purposes of all . . . . Effective leaders have a vision that

is persistent and consistent . . . . Commitment to a vision occurs only when people are actively involved in shaping it.[3]

Leaders and potential leaders can learn specific ideas and skills which can help them become "visionaries." They can learn how to communicate to their followers a very clear and definite picture of the future as they see and understand it. Symbols, examples, stories and analogies can be used to explain and illustrate their vision to followers. Involving others in an "envisioning process" helps build an institutional (e.g., parish) vision for the future. Leaders must learn and practice the virtue of persistence in refusing to abandon their dreams. A shared vision can sustain them to the end.

"Where there is no vision, the people perish." (Proverbs 29: 18)

Vision:
The foresight to lead the way and the capacity to communicate a dream that induces the commitment of followers. Vision gives life, form and vitality to the Church.

1. *Authority:*
It is the dream of the parish as an authority-leader to lead people by authorizing them to fulfill their official duties and obligations.

2. *Servant:*
It is the dream of the parish as a servant-leader to lead people to serve the highest priority needs of others.

3. *Community:*
It is the dream of the parish as a community-leader to lead unique people to share an ideal in a common life.

4. *Prophet:*
It is the dream of the parish as a prophet-leader to lead people to the truth by scrutinizing the signs of the times and interpreting them in the light of gospel values.

1. Authority

In the New Testament, all authority has been attributed to the Risen Christ, and all of the apostles were sent by Christ to preach the gospel with authority.

Jesus came forward and addressed the apostles in these words: full authority has been given to me both in heaven and on earth; go, therefore, and make disciples of all the nations. Baptize them in the name of the Father, the Son and the Holy Spirit. Teach them to carry out everything I have commanded you. And know that I am with you always, until the end of the world (Mt. 28: 18-20).

The apostles were given the responsibility and the right to speak authentically and authoritatively about something that they witnessed. They had first-hand knowledge about Christ and His teachings. They possessed the knowledge which is a fundamental source for human authority. Since they witnessed many events and facts, they were able to pass them on to others, and they to others in succession. This was the beginning of "apostolic succession."

Those in official positions in the Church also could interpret Christ's commandment to love one another as exactly that, i.e., a commandment. Consequently, it is their *duty* to love others; it is their *duty* to correct and reprimand those who sin or who err; it is their *duty* to pray, to worship, etc. To manifest one's love for another is to carry out one's authoritative duty and obligation. They have the right and the responsibility to protect the Church and "children" of Holy Mother Church.

Persons and parishes which emphasize this type of Church believe that the message of salvation was fulfilled and completed at the time of the Apostles. The contemporary Church must authentically and authoritatively proclaim the never-changing orthodoxy of Christ's Apostolic Church.

For I have not spoken on my own; no, the Father who sent me has commanded me what to say and how to speak. Since I know that His commandment means eternal life, whatever I say is spoken just as He instructed me (John 12: 49-50).

Parishes and leaders who have the authentic, apostolic spirit have the means by which they can instruct others to speak authoritatively about the traditional Church. The end product is to preserve the Church as founded by Christ and built by the apostles.

To govern in the Church is to use one's legitimate authority in relying on and reaffirming orthodoxy, defined dogma, approved liturgical celebrations, canon law and hierarchical decisions. To teach in the Church and about the Church means teaching the orthodoxy of the Church.

In his book, *Authority in the Church*, McKenzie writes that the New Testament identifies two features about authority. One is that the New Testament has little to say about authority. The other is that the New Testament is anti-authoritarian in the sense that it permits no member of the Church to occupy a position of dignity and eminence. The first in the Church must be the last; the first must be the servant of other people in the Church. No one should even desire an elevated status or rank in the Church. People must be dedicated to service in love.

> Authority in the Church must depart from the accepted forms of authority and find a new way to exercise itself. It must reflect the person and mission of Jesus Christ .... Authority in the Church belongs to the whole Church and not to particular officers. Authority is a gift of the Spirit .... Both the idea and the use of authority in the New Testament show no signs of rigorous control of the members by authority. Since the mission of the Church is the responsibility of all the members of the Church, all members have a concern in the exercise of authority.[4]

McKenzie goes on to say that what is needed in the Church is an examination of the use of authority. This is necessary, he says, because our contemporary world is much different from New Testament times. Even the contemporary corporate world has reformed its use of authority.

Nevertheless, ST (Sensing-Thinking) persons who value law and order, and are animated by an apostolic spirit have a vision for the Church which is consistent with their basic personality-type and basic Church-type. This mental concept of self and of Church leads them to behavioral patterns which they find comfortable and reliable. If they are Church leaders, they lead authoritatively. If they are Church followers, they prefer to be obedient. After all, the Church has survived beautifully for 2,000 years because of its apostolic spirit and its on-going authoritative vision. They believe that this Vision has been fulfilled and needs to be maintained.

2. Servant

In my opinion, Robert Greenleaf is today's preeminent expert and oracle for servant-leadership. He calls for individual leaders to be servant-leaders and says that institutions should be servant-leaders as well. It is his thesis that

> caring for persons, the more able and the less able serving each other, is the rock upon which a good society is built . . . . (that) servant-leaders are healers in the sense of making whole by helping others to a larger and nobler vision and purpose than they would be likely to attain for themselves . . . . (that) an institution is a gathering of persons who have accepted a common purpose, to the end that each involved person reaches higher fulfillment as a person, through serving and being served by the common venture, than would be achieved alone or in a less committed relationship.[5]

Caring is the essence of serving. Caring for the poor, the sick, the rich, the educated and the uneducated, the thirsty and hungry. Caring for all of God's children is service in action. To "serve the altar," to "serve the public" and to "serve our country" are examples of religious, political and military service. To "serve communion" and to preach God's word are examples of sacramental and heraldic service. In other words, service takes many forms and requires many ministries. In our interdependent, global world the Church attempts to serve international needs of justice, dignity, freedom and peace.

In order to achieve the Church's "diakonal" mission of building God's Kingdom here on earth, justice, dignity, freedom and peace must be used as its foundation blocks. The Christian servant-leader and the parish as servant-leader must begin by clearly communicating its dream and convincing people to actively hunger and thirst after justice.

There will be justice when men and women decide to act justly. The most basic need is the "transformation" of people, especially transforming those people who have some opportunity to influence the centers of power in society.

> Christians could make no greater contribution to domestic and international peace and justice than that of leading men and women to adopt those values and make those choices in which such peace and justice are rooted.[6]

Isaiah's "Suffering Servant" (Isaiah 52-53) and his fulfillment in the person of Christ indicate that the mission of the Church is to serve one another and to serve perfectly by giving one's life for another. However, it is by living for others that we serve one another best in today's society. By being "healers" we are able to serve. That is, persons who are physicians, therapists, counsellors, confessors, psychologists, parents, teachers, nurses, artists, politicians, etc. are serving by helping people become whole. As servant-leaders they help transform the lives of others. They believe with Christ that they "have come to serve and not to be served."

Persons and parishes serve by teaching and educating others. By teaching historical facts, technical skills and healthy attitudes, these servant-leaders serve the mind and intellect. By learning, people help themselves to be freer, healthier and wiser. In today's Church, people are needed to serve by becoming stewards of the Church's material possessions. Skillful persons are needed to build wisely, manage resources effectively, dispense goods justly and be fiscally responsible. Stewardship is a service that can free other Church leaders to use their skills and charisms to the advantage of the Church's mission.

SF (Sensing-Feeling) persons have an innate preference to care for people (feeling) by facing the facts (sensing) of the human condition in the world, and then to respond to people's needs by serving them. The "catholic" spirit of reaching out to everyone everywhere serves the Church well in fulfilling its catholic vision. Leaders who prefer and focus on a serving Church are usually realistic, practical and are able to provide resources to serve needy persons. Their pastoral approach is different from the ST authoritative approach. The ST persons may also provide service for people. However, they do so because it is their duty and obligation.

The SF people serve others because it is "natural" for them to do so. They feel for people and are natural servant-leaders.

3. Community

The word "community" connotes different meanings to different people. Community can refer to "humankind;" it can describe a parish, a diocese or a religous society. However, in our context it refers to a climate that is created when parishioners accept and follow a common ideal, and where people support one another. A common life could result from proclaiming a common ideal. The more time people spend together, the more committed they can become to common values. The concern they exhibit for one another indicates the vitality of their parish-community.

Leaders who are concerned primarily with organization, administration and authority usually are task-oriented, and they direct the work and energies of their followers to a common task. Leaders who are concerned primarily with service direct that work and those energies in a "supply and demand" service type of institution or parish-community. Leaders who are concerned primarily with forming and strengthening community focus their attentions on inter-personal relationships, rather than on programs, activities or service. The organizational aspect focuses on a gathering of people who form a strong, visible, supporting community. Its natural structure is one of communal relationships.

When forming a community, an ideal is needed to help motivate people toward such a vision. When the vision is to maintain and enhance a community that already exists, members of the community must be reminded about the original ideal which was the motivating factor. The ideal must remain important enough to warrant members' on-going commitment and active membership.

The ideal for the Church is Christ. In the book, *Building Christian Communities,* Clark says that:

> Christ is what is unique about Christianity. If what he did, his crucifixion, resurrection and ascension are not important for men to believe in and accept, then Christianity is not important . . . . The purpose of Christian community is to live for

> Christ . . . . How much importance do you place on forming a
> community in which life is formed around Christ, in which you
> will be helped to make Christ the first thing in your life? This
> is the issue which will decide the future of the Church.[6]

Community is important. It is through the experience of community,
the experience of belonging, that we are nourished in our faith, encouraged
to grow in our belief, and shown how to love. Like the Israelites we are
called to be a covenanted people, God's people in solidarity. We are
taught to be selfless in a selfish society. We are taught that we are brothers
and sisters in Christ. We learn that those who have a vision of community
have a yearning for cooperation, not competition; for sharing, not possess-
ing; for being committed to a common ideal, not alienated and lost.

In a communal climate people can interact with one another in caring
and nurturing ways that sustain a supportive and loving community life.
Unfortunately, too many religious communities, parishes and dioceses
have not recognized the contributions of its members, and heavy loss of
Church membership has been the consequence.

Archbishop Weakland emphasizes the importance of others in community in a context of economics. He says that:

> U.S. Catholics and other Americans are 'hyper-individualists'
> and this makes it difficult to preach economic justice to them
> . . . . The concept of the common good hardly means anything
> any more to many of our people . . . . I often take biblical pas-
> sages on dying to self and explain that you can't become a real
> disciple of Christ unless you are other-oriented.[7]

NF (iNtuitive-Feeling) persons are concerned about possibilities and the
future (N), and about people, values and feeling (F). They are idealists.
Nothing is impossible for them. They feel that they must be sensitive to
the feelings of all people. They have strong convictions (ideals) and
desperately want to respond to the needs of people in the community.
Since they are idealists they tend to measure their successes against rigid
standards of perfection instead of what is real and possible. Seeking the
ideal community is important because people will have an opportunity to

share an ideal. They will have opportunities to be commonly involved with people and their personal values.

In the end, the formation of the community of faith remains the work of the Spirit. A well-structured group that is clear in its goals, open in its communication, and committed to its religious values may still founder. Life remains that ambiguous; faith, that much a mystery. But the person who is aware of the social dynamics of group life and sensitive to the purpose and particular history of *this* group can contribute importantly to the possibility of community. And the possibility of community is the hope in which we stand, awaiting the gracious visitation of our God.[8]

4. Prophet

Prophets are spokespersons for God. Throughout history their messages all converge to form the same consistent message which is the revelation of God's plan for His people. In the Old Testament the meaning of the covenant was always being interpreted by the prophet for contemporary man and woman. This was the essential and most important duty of the prophet. It was the prophet's responsibility to point out the deeper significance of God's message, to help people focus more clearly on those realities which were always implicit but which they could not fully understand. Essentially, prophets interpret, get at the deeper meaning and point the way.

Just as a sacrament is a sign, so too is a prophet a sign; someone who points the way to Christ. A sign can be a pointer to something that is absent. It is in this sense that the prophet usually spoke. The prophet usually was very unpopular because the message usually "shocked" people. The sins and deficiencies of society were pointed out. Dissonant notes were being played and the listeners did not want to "face the music." Amos, Jeremias, Ezekiel, Isaiah and all the Old Testament prophets pointed to the ills of society and told the people to reform, to return to lives consistent with the expectations of the covenant.

Contemporary prophets have the same charism of scrutinizing the signs of the times. It is a charism of knowledge, wisdom, discernment and courage. A special charism moves men and women to analyze and critique themselves, the Church and society. They remind people that God's love is always available to everyone at all times.

Just as prophets were not accepted by officials in the New Testament, and just as prophets were not readily accepted by officials throughout the history of the Church (e.g., Joan of Arc, Catherine of Siena, Francis of Assisi, Thomas More, Teilhard de Chardin), so too relations between present-day prophets and officials are usually hostile.

Prophets issue warnings, make threats, utter promises or extend blessings—whatever it takes—to awaken people from their present malaise or sinful ways. Usually it is the leader (president, king, governor, pope) who is being warned, threatened, praised or blessed. The failure of the Church or any institution is usually blamed for the failure of leadership. Consequently, it is the leader who takes the heat from the prophet.

Besides being one who spoke with authority, who reached out to everyone everywhere, who formed a community of apostles, Jesus was a prophet also.

> . . . Jesus exhibits all the features of the prophet. He spoke the word of God; he uttered denunciations and promises; and he stood outside the hierarchical structure of Judaism. If the Church does not exercise the prophetic office, she fails to carry on a part of the mission of Jesus.[9]

Prophets are important to the Church because, at times, they point to some officials of the Church who do not speak or act as the Holy Spirit would have them. Prophets are uncontrollable because they are empowered by the Holy Spirit who has not been able to move official authorities to hear the same message being given to the prophet. The authority-type leaders feel more comfortable and secure when they rely on their own authority.

In addition, prophets are important to the Church because they are change-agents who will not permit the Church to stagnate in mediocrity or callousness for very long. Reform and renewal are difficult changes for individuals and parishes because stability may be mistaken for rigidity, unity may be mistaken for uniformity, organization may be mistaken for institutionalism, authority may be mistaken for autocracy. Authentic prophecy exists for the purpose of restructuring, reorganizing, revitalizing and re-forming the community so that it remains true to the gospels while remaining relevant to the lives of God's people.

In regard to the specific signs of the times that have been scrutinized by the U.S. bishops in their prophetic *A Shepherd's Care,* a major goal for diocesan and parish leaders will be to build and rebuild parish communities that can provide for the basic needs of Catholics to live Christian lives. The climate of the parish community must be such that it helps form parishioners' values, feelings, attitudes, faith and life styles. By being members of parishes which are alive, parishioners will be immersed in a climate that will nourish and support them in living strong and vibrant lives. On the other hand, parishes that are not alive and vibrant will have little effect in influencing the individual lives of persons or the life of the community where the parish is located. In these cases the prophet-leader, the individual and the parish, must lead the way in calling for revitalization and reorganization.

In those dioceses where a prophet-bishop is proposing change:

• Parishioners must perceive that the contemplated changes are positive, and that they have the potential for producing positive results for the parishioners.

• Prophet-leaders are change agents. They must realize that change is a process that has to evolve. It cannot be rushed and must be given time to unfold. Renewal, revitalization and restructuring cannot happen quickly by legislation, or by letters from the bishop or pastor, or by conducting a few workshops and seminars.

• Leaders must view change as a personal experience. People affected by change feel it personally and need time to emote. Change agents cannot ignore or deny the feelings of people. They must attend to them.

• Leaders of change must realize that the individual person is the focal point in any change effort. Even though persons are members of a parish organization they will always be individual persons. For leaders, this means that they must be aware of what is happening to both the individual parishioner and all of the parishioners collectively as a parish.

• Leaders of change must gain acceptance for their change project. Trust and credibility are the keys for acceptance.

• Parishioners must feel that what is being proposed and what will be accomplished is truly for their benefit as well as for the benefit of the diocese. Tension will definitely occur when there is a tug between retaining individual autonomy and diocesan constraints.

• On-going inservice programs for parish leaders are needed to build awareness and skills so that people on the local parish level will have ownership, and that they will know that they are invited to actively participate in the change efforts for personal and parish revitalization and reorganization.

• Substantial change in individual persons rarely happens without group processes that provide for mutual support, healthy exchange of feelings and ideas, problem solving opportunities, and time to maintain and develop enthusiasm in people.

Few people enjoy the presence of prophets who call for change. Most people feel uncomfortable and uneasy, and naturally so. However, there is a need for healthy tension between the prophet's criticism and common beliefs and practices. If we see the prophets as parishes and persons who take a hard, long look at what is wrong with our Church, our government, our institutions and what is needed to set it right again, we will see the importance and necessity of prophets in our contemporary society.

Prophets shock people. Their message can be disconcerting. By reminding people of God's real message they empower people to reform their lives and institutions, and raise themselves up. As change agents, they can help parishes revitalize and reorganize in order to develop environments where people can renew their lives.

Throughout history prophets were almost always killed by the people who did not want to hear the truth. In today's world the prophets are rarely killed. They are usually ignored, laughed at and criticized. The Church, as prophet, may feel that it is being ignored and laughed at and unduly criticized in today's highly materialistic world. Nevertheless, the prophets must speak.

From a typological perspective, NT (iNtuitive-Thinking) persons are concerned primarily with possibilities for the future (N) and achieving them through logical (T) planning projects. They are the agents for change, architects for new organizational structures. Usually, they can read the signs of oncoming change and can be creative, innovative and ingenious in planning for change. Because they tend to live their lives in the future, they do not enjoy traditions and customs. They prefer to change them.

As "Thinkers" they love to analyze and organize, and to renew what needs to be renewed. In pointing out dissonance and flaws, NTs can stand firm for what they believe in. Consequently, they seem to have a propensity to be disconcerting. They believe they are empowering organizations and individual persons to be true to themselves by challenging them, by pointing to the "truth." In this sense, they are usually the ones who are calling the Church to be holy and distinct. Their values are congruent with their vision. The parish, as a prophet Church, must call itself to holiness and to distinction.

The Church is at the same time holy and always in need of being purified, and incessantly pursues the path of penance and renewal.[10]

Summary

This is a brief summary of the ideas about Persons, Spirit and Vision. Jesus was a person who exemplified what a leader should be, and what the Church should be like as a leader. He spoke and acted with authority and authenticity. He served all of the people, Jew and Gentile, rich and poor, educated and uneducated, believers and unbelievers. He formed a community of apostles and disciples. He united them through personal relationships and shared beliefs. They were persons and a Church of distinction, re-formed and renewed into a new institution of Christians.

As baptized persons, Christians were called forth to use their charisms within the Church-community to fulfill the variety of needs of diverse people. Individuals exercised their unique charisms to preach, teach, serve, prophesy, administer, etc. in building the institution of the Church. They used their power as individual persons and collectively as the Church to impact the feeling, thinking and behavior of others which has produced lasting results for the world. In fact, their Spirit and Vision have given life, form and vitality to an institution: the Catholic Church and our parishes.

7

A Miracle Is Needed In Every Parish: Shared Power

When some of my friends and I discussed the concept of power in the context of leadership, the remarks were quite spontaneous and insightful. And, they displayed a whole power spectrum. Church leadership is corrupted when it is thought of in terms of power, said one. Bureaucratic power corrupts more than any other form of power. Another said that the call to preach the word and to celebrate the sacraments is a call to powerlessness; that the Church's ministers should be persons without power living in the name of the Lord.

Power is seen also as a reality of life, especially organizational life. The effective use of power, said another friend, is a necessary and critical function in a Church with authority and influence. On the one hand it is necessary. On the other hand it is to be distrusted. Someone quoted Henry Kissinger as saying that "power is the great aphrodisiac."

What do the researchers and experts say about power? Bennis says that "leadership is, quite simply, the wise use of power . . . and, power is the capacity to translate intention into reality and sustain it."[1] Greenleaf thinks that ". . . power is used to create opportunity and alternatives so that individuals may choose and build autonomy."[2] Bennis also believes that

> we need to establish a new tradition in the workplace—a tradition of mutual trust and shared enterprise in which managers share power and become accountable to workers, and

employees are willing to accept the risks along with the rewards of participation.[3]

Leadership is seen by some as a reaching out; that it holds people accountable; it tells the truth and it tries to use power to empower and authority to authorize. Leaders discover over and over again that releasing power to others benefits them in the long run. The more they empower others the more they can achieve, and the entire enterprise becomes more successful. Likert noted that "participative management systems stimulate leadership behavior from subordinates . . . ."[4]

Leaders who are able to develop strong leaders in their organizations by helping them to appreciate their own charisms as persons can create stronger organizations. Leaders who develop leaders are empowering them. They call forth rather than control. Leaders don't invent motivation in others; they unlock it. They tap the motives in others that serve the purposes of the group in the organization. They pursue shared goals. Collaboration and joint determination are the watchwords for the most productive use of leadership power. Leaders, no matter the level or background of their workers or the nature of the work, can best meet individual and organizational needs by sharing power through participation.

In their classic work on power, Mouton and Blake studied the different consequences of different uses of power. They discovered that the most effective leaders best fulfill the needs of individuals and of the organization by sharing power. They do this by inviting others to participate.

> . . . the effects of power sharing through participation have no discernible limits of application . . . . The research spectrum is so broad and the conclusions so complementary that it would be difficult for any manager to claim that any situation or subordinate were so unique that participative practices would not produce similar results . . . . The use of such a simple and uncontrolling method as participation seems . . . as some sort of managerial miracle. Without undue exaggeration, the results achieved can also be termed miraculous.[5]

This use of power applies universally in all work situations with all workers, including the work of the Lord and His workers.

Boff adds his thoughts about how power should be shared in the context of Church.

> The exercise of shared coresponsibility must be thought out, developed, and organized, with reference to specific missions within the pastoral plan of the hierarchy. Lay people today are more sensitive to real participation where decisions are being made. There is the desire to not simply offer suggestions to those who decide but to decide together with them.[6]

Power in the Bible

In the Bible power is morally neutral. Power is used to cause both good and evil things to happen. We read in the Bible that God manifests power through agents. For example, in the Book of Exodus, nature (locusts, the sea, etc.) is an agent used by God to free His people from captivity. Persons, individually and corporately, are agents also. However, unlike nature, they are moral agents. Moses, David, Solomon, Judas, Peter and Pilate, for example, received power from God to make an impact on the feeling, thinking and behavior of their followers. They were successful when they recognized the power they possessed as coming from God. (Jesus told Pilate that he would have no power if it did not come from the heavenly Father above.)

When did they fail? Moses doubted the power of God to produce water from a rock. David used the power of his "office" to manipulate a soldier in order to satisfy his lust for the soldier's wife. Solomon used self-serving power for fame and riches. Judas used his power as treasurer to cheat, lie and betray. Peter was afraid to trust in the power of Christ's love. Pilate had more faith in the power of the Roman Empire than he had in the loving power of Christ.

At times, persons and institutions substitute for the power of love the power of money, social position, control, domination, sex, military control, political clout, intellectual superiority or physical strength. Self-serving power corrupts love. Bureaucratic power probably corrupts love more than any other kind of power. Self-serving power is described in the devil's temptation of Jesus in the desert. Isn't this kind of self-serving, corrupting power being portrayed in today's culture as normal and desirable? In other words, like Christ, we are being tempted to worship the devil in a world that prefers temporary riches to eternal values, material possessions to heavenly rewards.

> Then Jesus was led into the desert by the Spirit to be tempted by the devil. He fasted forty days and forty nights, and afterward was hungry. The tempter approached and said to him, "If you are the Son of God, command these stones to turn into bread." Jesus replied, "Scripture has it: Not on bread alone is man to live, but on every utterance that comes from the mouth of God."

> Next the devil took him to the holy city, set him on the parapet of the temple, and said, "If you are the Son of God, throw yourself down. Scripture has it: He will bid his angels take care of you; with their hands they will support you that you may never stumble on a stone."

> Jesus answered him, "Scripture also has it: You shall not put the Lord your God to the test."

> The devil then took him up a very high mountain and displayed before him all the kingdoms of the world in their magnificence, promising, "All these will I bestow on you if you prostrate yourself in homage before me." At this, Jesus said to him, "Away with you, Satan! Scripture has it: You shall do homage to the Lord your God; him alone shall you adore."

> At that the devil left him, and angels came and waited on him.

> —Matthew 4: 1-11.

The spirit of darkness tries to vanquish Jesus. He shows Christ all the kingdoms of the world. He tempts Jesus with all the world's riches, glory and splendor. How tempting this could be for someone who is ambitious, for someone who believes and pretends to be a "Savior." Hitler, Idi Amin, Mussolini, Stalin are a few extreme examples of men possessed—by power. Or was it the devil? Or is corrupting power really the devil?

The devil knows human nature. He knows that those who have attained a high degree of perfection and of union with God, can often be above the reach of the sensual appetites, but can be seduced by more subtle suggestions of pride and presumption. They can believe themselves to be better than others, and think that God owes them because of their faithfulness. The devil tries to tempt Christ in this way. If Jesus is the Son of God, what a miraculous proof of His omnipotent power, what an obvious sign that God is with Him if He were to appear suddenly from above and dramatically appear to the people in the crowded temple court!

Jesus rejected the devil and his temptations that can make corrupting, self-serving power look so attractive and desirable.

Sacred Scripture offers further clarification of Jesus' attitude toward power and leadership:

In Matthew, Jesus called the disciples together and said,

> You know how those who exercise authority among the Gentiles lord it over them. Their great ones make their importance felt. It cannot be like that with you. Anyone among you who aspires to greatness must serve the rest; whoever wants to rank first must serve the needs of all.

In Luke, Jesus said,

> Earthly kings lord it over their people. Who in fact is greater? He who reclines at table, or he who serves the meal? Is not the one who reclines at table? Yet I am in your midst as one who serves you.

In John's gospel:

> If I wash your feet, I who am teacher and Lord, then you must wash each others' feet. What I just did was to give you an example.

In Matthew, when Jesus said, "Whatever you declare bound on earth shall be bound in heaven, and whatever you declare loosed on earth shall be loosed in heaven," he was referring to the plural "you," the community, not to Peter as head of the Church. He was suggesting that there is a communal way of behaving. In this example the parish community is expected to act as leader. And all the baptized in a parish constitute the parish community.

> Jesus did not proclaim an established order; he did not call others to be rulers but to be submissive, humble, and loyal. He liberates for freedom and love that allow one to be submissive yet free, critical, and loyal without being servile, that call those in power to be servants and brothers free from the appetite for greater power . . . . What is the power of God? It is the power of love. The power of love is different in nature from the power of domination.[7]

What Motivates Leaders To Use Power?

Popes, presidents, parents, prime ministers, paupers, pastors and politicians have relative degrees of power to impact persons in their own worlds. However, why do they use that power? What motivates them, as moral agents, to do good or evil?

We have summarized a list of specific tendencies that motivate leaders. We would hope that, in checking this list, Church leaders, indeed all leaders—parents, boy scout leaders, office managers, pastors, educators, CEOs, parish council members, politicians, anyone who wants to influence the behavior of other people—may better understand how to use power wisely and lovingly.

Power impacts the behavior of other people. It can be corrupt, selfish, self-aggrandizing and personally rewarding. Leaders who use power for these purposes are motivated by self-serving tendencies. They are not using power wisely or lovingly. On the other hand, power can be love-giving, selfless, influencing the common good, fulfilling the priority needs of individuals and organizations. Leaders who use power for these purposes are motivated by love-giving tendencies. They are using power wisely and lovingly.

Leaders do have certain power tendencies. They are innately and environmentally acquired and constitute a powerful motivating force. They use power based on their interior motivations which are either SELF-SERVING or LOVE-GIVING.

(See figure 1, pp. 83-84, and complete the exercise "Power Tendencies of Leaders" to check your motivational tendencies.)

This list can help leaders identify the motivations behind their use of power and help them and their followers know why they act as they do. This list can be used as criteria to help us evaluate whether we are using our leadership power for others or really to serve our own purposes.

When a Person Cooperates With Grace the Power of Love Is Produced

When we are motivated by loving tendencies to use our natural talents to make positive impacts on the common good, we are cooperating with the grace of God. Through grace we are empowered by God to develop our charisms in order to build up nature, to do good, to beautify, to love, to serve, to grow in knowledge and wisdom, to form caring communities, to transform society. Actual, or helping, grace refers to the help that the Holy Spirit gives us to perform all of the above acts of good will for others. Grace describes the Spirit's actions which produce the power of love.

Power Tendencies of Leaders (figure 1)

Life-Giving Tendencies	*Self-Serving Tendencies*
___ desire power for the purpose of impacting the behavior of others for the common good.	___ desire power for the purpose of impacting the behavior of others for personal gain.
___ treat people as valuable, and as capable of contributing to parish problem solving and decision making.	___ treat people as objects who should conform and obey.
___ make others feel strong, not weak.	___ make others feel weak and powerless.
___ release power to others.	___ restrict power to selves.

___ share power through participation.	___ use authority and coercion.
___ exhibit self-control and inhibition in their use of power.	___ exhibit impulsiveness and erratic use of power.
___ show respect for others.	___ disrespectful & overbearing.
___ focus on fairness.	___ manipulative & exploitative.
___ concerned with justice.	___ focus on control & strength.
___ value work.	___ value efficiency.
___ concerned with equal rights.	___ selfish.
___ ambivalent about power.	___ excited about use of power.
___ goals are realistic, yet challenging.	___ goals are unrealistic and exceptionally high.
___ collaborative.	___ competitive.
___ open, non-defensive and willing to seek help from others.	___ closed, defensive and exhibit sense of self-importance.
___ others receive support and strength from them.	___ others depend on them for direction, control and expertise.
___ when leaving organization, system is intact and self-sustaining.	___ when leaving organization, they are difficult to replace.

When persons use power that is motivated by love-giving tendencies, they cooperate with grace. These are institutions and individuals who desire power for the purpose of impacting the behavior of others for the common good. When they use power that is motivated by self-serving tendencies they are not cooperating with grace. These are the leaders who desire power for the purpose of impacting the behavior of others for their own personal gain.

When persons and parishes consciously decide to permit the Holy Spirit to help them perform acts of good will for the common good their individual and collective natural gifts (charisms) combined with the power of grace are transformed and shaped into a power of love.

If we were to use the jargon of typology to describe the phenomenon of grace, we would say the following:

> The archetypes choose us, as much as or more than we choose the archetypes. This is another way to speak of what Christian theology calls 'grace,' the grace of vocation, or the gifts of the Spirit.[8]

Power is a dynamic activity. That dynamic activity can be the activity of love or the activity of domination. Personal and institutional power, just like the power of the atom, can be harnessed and mobilized for building up or tearing down. Power can be used by God's moral agents to fulfill the devil's agenda for personal and global corruption, destruction and holocaust (e.g., Stalin, Hitler, Mussolini, KKK, the Nazi government). Or, the power of love can be used to produce lasting, loving results for the world (Jesus, St. Francis, Mother Theresa, a parish, the Church).

Shared Power Is Love

As a result of the above discussion about power, we have come to the conclusion that the most worthwhile and effective kind of power in communities, institutions, families, parishes, etc. is shared power.

SHARED POWER is that activity of person(s) which impacts the feeling, thinking and behavior of other persons and produces lasting results for parishes and parishioners.

Our concept of "activity" refers to a person's inherent powers (charisms) that bring about change in a person or a situation. It also refers to an entire parish of persons with a collective network of charisms. Love *is* that active power in a person. To love is to share, to give. It does not mean that a person must give up something or give in to somebody.

Giving should not be understood as depriving oneself of something for the sake of another. Rather, in giving we should experience the power and productivity of our talents and charisms. Sharing the power of our charisms indicates that we are alive and that we are able to bring to life the potentialities of others. It means that love is both cause and effect.

Some people may be surprised at what Karl Marx said about love.

> If you love without calling forth love, that is, if your love as such does not produce love, if by means of an expression of life as a loving person you do not make yourself a loved person, then your love is impotent, a misfortune.[9]

Love must be a giving and productive love. Fromm says that:

> beyond the element of giving, the active character of love becomes evident in the fact that it always implies certain basic elements common to all forms of love. These are *care, responsibility, respect and knowledge.*[10]

If a parent (leader) does not *care* for a child by not demonstrating an on-going active concern for him or her, we would quickly make the valid judgment that the parent does not love the child. Parents are leaders who must show their love through the constant care of the one they love. Politicians, teachers and all leaders must exhibit that same essential quality of care for those "in their care," both for individual persons and institutions.

A good parent works hard at helping a child grow. A teacher works hard at helping a child grow intellectually. A pastor works hard at helping a child grow spiritually. Work and growth are the keystones of caring. As Fromm says,

> The essence of love is to 'labor' for something and 'to make something grow,' . . . . One loves that for which one labors, and one labors for that which one loves.[11]

Responsibility can be understood as fulfilling one's duty. In the sense used here, responsibility is a voluntary action. It means that a person is ready, willing and capable of responding to the needs of others. All leaders, to be effective, must assume this threefold posture of preparation and be actively and willingly responsible for their brothers and sisters in the world.

To *respect* people and institutions is to look at them as they are (from the latin word, "respicere"). It means that persons should develop and grow naturally without leaders exploiting and manipulating them for their own purposes. It means that parishes should evolve and grow in response to their authentic purpose, and be able to offer relevant and meaningful services to help fulfill the real needs of people and the expectations of the Church.

Knowledge is the fourth charismatic element of love according to Fromm.

> To respect a person is not possible without knowing him; care and responsibility would be blind if they were not guided by knowledge. Knowledge would be empty if it were not motivated by concern.[12]

Moreover, there are different kinds of knowledge: knowledge of self, knowing others, knowledge about things and events in the world, the knowledge of the past, etc.

> Care, responsibility, respect and knowledge are mutually interdependent. They are a syndrome of attitudes which are to be found in the mature person; that is, in the person who develops his own powers productively, who only wants to have that which he has worked for . . . who has acquired humility based on the inner strength which only genuine productivity can give.[13]

Care, responsibility, respect and knowledge are special charisms, personal talents freely given by God. Individuals are expected to develop and use them in the productive service of fulfilling the needs of others in the community. When leaders invite people to use their charisms in service to others in the community they are empowering them to be giving and productive. A parish begins to form a sense of community when it coordinates the charisms of its parishioners in service to the community.

The laity can also feel themselves called, or be called, to work with their pastors in the service of the ecclesial community, for its growth and life, by exercising a great variety of ministries according to the grace and charisms which the Lord is pleased to give them.[14]

According to typology, once again, which is the reference point of the Leadership Paradigm, the element of knowledge is a special charism or power of the ST personality-type; care is a special charism or power of the SF type; respect is a special charism or power of the NT type; and, responsibility is a special charism or power of the NF type.

Each type may possess other charisms as well. However, they possess one special charism that is a dominant strength. According to persons who study personality-typology, persons usually possess a second charism which is called an auxiliary strength.

We also believe that each leadership-type spontaneously calls forth and taps from others that special charism, that element of love, which is natural to their own types, and which appeals to them in other people. We believe that the healthy leadership-type is able to call forth from themselves and others whatever charism is needed at that particular moment to have the greatest and most beneficial impact on people. For instance, the healthy leader is one who is able to use the charism of knowledge when he/she needs it. He/she is able to use the charism of caring when it is needed, and so on with the other charisms. However, we must admit that it is difficult for one person to be all things to all people.

The most effective leaders, both corporate and individual, have the capacity to use all four basic types of power which are described here below. Nevertheless, because our human nature is what it is, each person prefers to use one or two types of power and is very good at it. Usually, they are not good at using one or two of the other types of power.

The Four Basic Types of Power

1. THE POWER OF KNOWLEDGE

Sensing-Thinking (ST) leaders rely primarily on the power of knowledge. They use this charism to impact their followers. As leaders, they are good administrators who use their "office" to emphasize control, direction and loyalty to an institution with an authority hierarchy. They know their personnel. They know the rules. They know the facts. They expect their followers to know the facts and the rules. They use authority to authorize policies and fixed procedures. They envision an institution which maintains law, order, customs and traditions. The type of parish which relies primarily on this type of power has the same characteristics.

2. THE POWER OF CARE

Sensing-Feeling (SF) leaders use their power of caring to serve, at once, the institution and the individual members of the institution. Servant-leaders rely on the charism of caring to impact others. Because they care about both, the individual and the institution, tasks and persons, product and process, efficiency and human relations are usually addressed. They try to influence their followers by establishing humane conditions for them to accomplish their work. The type of parish which relies primarily on this type of power has the same characteristics.

3. THE POWER OF RESPONSIBILITY

Intuitive-Feeling (NF) community-leaders feel that they have the responsibility to form a community spirit or a community where people are able to establish personal relationships. They impact their followers with the belief that they are created in God's image and likeness, that they have been given free will, and that they are made free by Christ's death and resurrection. Based on these beliefs and using their special charism of feeling responsible for others, they try to free people to be mutually responsible for one another in a community where they live out their shared common values. The type of parish which relies primarily on this type of power has the same characteristics.

4. THE POWER OF RESPECT

Intuitive-Thinking (NT) prophet-leaders rely on the power of respect. That is, "they look into" contemporary society in order to determine what changes are needed. They also have the charism of recognizing the talents of other people. They usually invite them to be colleagues in reforming whatever needs to be changed. They try to influence their followers by calling for renewal, which can be personal growth and communal revitalization.

Empowering-Productive Leaders

We believe very strongly that the most effective leaders are the ones who are able to share their power. The most effective parishes are able to coordinate and mobilize the different types of power. Sharing power (sharing knowledge, care, responsibility and respect), and giving all persons opportunities to use these charisms are not new ideas. They are found in Sacred Scripture. They are sound theological principles. They are practical and effective pastoral practices. They work in every human situation: in families, corporate offices, symphony orchestras, coal mines, baseball teams, ranches, parish councils and parishes.

Stated simply, shared responsibility (which also has been described as collegiality, co-responsibility and participatory involvement) means that each member of the Church, by reason of baptism, has the right and the duty to participate in the Church's mission to make Christ present here on earth and to speak the liberating truth of His Good News.[15]

Vatican Council II provides us with an enlightened understanding of the sacraments of initiation: baptism and confirmation. All the baptized and confirmed form a community of equals. Sacred Scripture supports this claim in Matthew 23: 8, i.e., there is a basic equality in the Church because we are all brothers and sisters baptized in Christ and anointed with the Holy Spirit. In that community all baptized persons are leaders in different ways according to their vocation, ministry and mission.

All baptized Catholics—poor and rich, educated and uneducated, politically powerful and powerless—are empowered through baptism to use their charisms, resources, energy and time to help fulfill the mission of Christ in the world.

By baptism all are leaders. All have power. All leaders possess talents and charisms which can be used to build up communities and individuals.

For parishes to share power (the powers of knowledge, care, responsibility and respect) is to empower baptized persons to participate in making decisions about those matters which directly affect their lives. To invite people to share all of their charisms is to empower persons to produce success in building the Kingdom of God here on earth. Parishes would be wise to follow the example of the Triune God who empowers all creatures. This is true because God creates all persons in His image and likeness, with intellect and free will, liberated by the Son of God, and daily animated by the Holy Spirit to help us renew the face of the earth.

Parishes which empower call forth rather than control their followers. They unlock the storehouse of talents, charisms, skills and competencies in each individual follower. They tap them to serve the purposes of the Church in the pursuit of a shared vision. They release the power of love which was poured forth into the hearts of every person at baptism and confirmation. They communicate the feeling to their followers that they are significant and make a difference. People are given the opportunity to learn and develop on the job. People have a sense of belonging, a connectedness, a feeling of being joined together in a common venture which is serious, but also fun. When they are empowered, people feel so involved in their game of work that they forget some of their basic needs for long periods of time. They are empowered to be themselves, to be equal members of the Church, and to be all that they can be. They are empowered to be productive co-leaders.

Empowering parishes assures productivity. Empowering and productive parishes create a climate that permits every person to make his or her maximum contribution. By creating this empowering-productive climate, parishes create opportunities for people to do wonderful and great things with the power of their own charisms, working together in synergy with others. When the followers are committed co-owners of the Church enterprise they feel fulfilled and want to fulfill the goals of the Church. Empowering-productive parishes are strong and decisive, yet sensitive to their followers to the degree of including them in decision making processes which directly affect their lives. They somehow create channels to hear everyone's viewpoint and give everyone a fair shake. When leaders can do the above, people feel a part of something "miraculous." As Mouton and Blake have observed, miraculous results occur. Shared power produces love.

A Miracle Is Needed in the Parish

The miracle that is needed in today's parish and Church is exactly what the Bible, Vatican Council II, scholarly research, human experience and divine example call for. The Church, the People of God, must exercise the simple and uncontrolling method of participation. Jay Dolan points out how Vatican II emphasized a participatory style which has produced changes in the Church.

> Once the Second Vatican Council sanctified the principle of participation of the people in the liturgy, the celebration of Mass and the sacraments were destined to change. The moment the Council defined the Church as the people of God, a change in thinking took place and eventually a change in acting as well; the concept of shared responsibility entered in to Church life and with it came shared decision-making. These changes have been developing for close to 20 years . . . .[16]

In sharing power with all the baptized members, the needs of parish members are best fulfilled, and the expectations of the parish as an institution are best met. *The Notre Dame Study of Catholic Life Since Vatican II* corroborates this point emphatically:

Participation ranked at the top of reasons pastors and administrators cited for the presence of vitality in their parishes
. . . . The best place to see the new church participation is in
the liturgy itself . . . . Another expression of lay people's increased sense of ownership of the church is the degree to
which they now lead it at the parish level.[17]

8

A Parish Is Expected To Produce Miraculous Results

> A good tree does not produce decayed fruit any more than a decayed tree produces good fruit. Each tree is known by its yield (Luke 7: 43-44).

When parishioners are empowered to participate in the parish, they are being called to produce a "yield:" i.e., lasting and loving results for themselves and for their parishes.

Empowering love is acknowledging and calling forth individual parishioners to use their unique charisms. Some readers may recognize this as "vocation." Secondly, productive-love is the actual use of charisms in service to others. This, of course, is productive for the parish community, the local community and the Church. Productive-love, then, is the use of charisms in actual service to others. Some readers may recognize this as "ministry."

> Christian ministry is the public activity of a baptized follower of Jesus Christ flowing from the Spirit's charism and an individual personality on behalf of a Christian community to witness to, serve and realize the Kingdom of God.[1]

When parishioners use the empowering love that comes from their vocation and use it productively in ministry to others, they feel fulfilled and loved. They express their love for others by serving them. They gain self-esteem and are able to love themselves in a healthy way. They are fulfilling the biblical mandate: "Love your neighbor as yourself." And, as Fromm says:

> From this it follows that my own self must be as much an object of my love as another person. The affirmation of one's own life, happiness, growth, freedom is rooted in one's capacity to love, i.e., in care, respect, responsibility, and knowledge. If an individual is able to love productively, he loves himself too . . . .[2]

Empowering-love happens when parishes recognize the charisms of others and commission them to use their charisms. Individual persons feel fulfilled. They feel loved. They feel good about themselves.

When parish leaders empower others to use their charisms to help fulfill the mission of the parish community, love produces love. Parishioners do this by using their charisms to produce good things for the parish and for the community. They become co-leaders through shared power. They feel that they are valuable and productive partners and co-owners of a shared enterprise.

What is the mission of the parish community? What is the purpose of a parish in today's world? What is a parish trying to accomplish? What is Christ's mission in the world? How do parishes and parish leaders build God's Kingdom in the world? What are the results that parish leaders and parishes intend to produce for individuals, parishes and communities?

The Constitution on the Church in the Modern World answers these questions by stating that the purpose of the Church is that "the kingdom of God may come and the salvation of the human race may be accomplished."[3] The primary mission of the Catholic Church in the world is to continue to build and expand the Kingdom of God. In actuality, to build God's Kingdom includes a variety of missions: caring for the aged, the lonely, the hungry, the homeless, the poor; administering the sacraments, participating in the liturgy; promoting justice and peace; healing the sick; teaching the ten commandments, the laws of the Church, medical ethics and bioethics; governing, teaching and serving, etc., etc. The list is endless. This list addresses *what* the specific missions are. It addresses the question, "What are we sent to do as individuals and as a parish community?"

Empowering others and coordinating their charisms in parish ministries is the way we go about building the kingdom. The four "miraculous results" of these synergistic efforts on a parish level are the *formation* of parish community, its ability to *transform* the lives of people, *informing* people about the unchanging gospels and constantly *re-forming* the Church and its parishes to fit the changing needs of people in their contemporary cultures. The most effective way to achieve these miraculous results is to empower parishioners to participate in shaping and forming the parish community and, with it, the kingdom of God.

```
               form
              /    \
        reform      inform
              \    /
            transform
```

I planted the seed	(formation)
and Apollos watered it	(information)
but God made it grow.	(transformation and re-formation)
(1 Cor. 3:6)	

1. To *form* a parish community is to produce a local network of baptized persons whose faith is publicly demonstrated in its four principal functions as a parish:

Worshiping parish community;

Servicing parish community;

Administering parish community;

Educating parish community.

A parishioner's faith is personally believed and lived out in a variety of ministries to others in the parish community. By responding to the needs of individual parishioners who desire personal relationships, a sense of community can be formed. Within the parish community parishioners have opportunities to respond to one another's needs. Additionally, parish ministries must reach out beyond the parish community and touch non-parishioners in the larger community. In fact, the parish shares in the larger role of the Church as diocese and universal Church.

As American Catholics, we value the opportunities to express ourselves as unique individuals while feeling the need to work side by side, in teamwork and cooperation, and to live in harmony and community with people of diverse creeds, colors and races.

To be a caring parish community, parishioners must have a sense of belonging, fellowship, solidarity, social cohesion, shared values, shared vision, a recognition of charisms, and the ability to work together and to respond to one another's needs. And, a parish community welcomes and unites diverse types of people.

> One of the reasons a group begins to form is because they recognize similarities: 'These people are like me.' Coping with diversity for a homogeneous group will be a bigger problem. A community must seek diversity of experiences, interests, orientation, skills, age or values. Communities require diversity and pluralism to ensure their growth, survival and effectiveness.[4]

A parish community performs a variety of good works for its parishioners and for others when it worships, educates, administers and serves. These good works are carried out through parish ministries in the community.

> . . . faith without works is dead as a body without breath
> (James 2: 26).

2. *Information* is a result of sharing knowledge. When parishes share knowledge, parishioners are informed. This information is about what to believe and how to live. Parishes have a lasting effect on people by giving them knowledge. Individuals feel fulfilled and satisfied because they have been empowered with information. The gospels are shared with everyone; Church teachings are taught; important information about spiritual and temporal matters are shared.

Parishes must empower and encourage people to share their knowledge with others. This assures stability and continuity for the Church. They help the Church fulfill its goals by focusing their love on the authentic Church of the past, and making certain that the Church has a future.

When parishes share the power of knowledge, the specific result is information. For instance, when families share knowledge about family traditions, their roots, their work at the office or factory, and about their family values they open up a storehouse of information for their children. By sharing important facts, feelings and information, family members build an information base for making decisions, for solving problems, for dreaming dreams, and for living their lives.

Leaders of any kind of organization perform the same function for their workers. By sharing pieces of knowledge about company policies, philosophy, values, profits, deficits, needed changes, etc., people have information they need to function and work effectively and efficiently. If people do not have the information they need to meet specific expectations, there is a breakdown in morale, job satisfaction, and in productivity and sensitivity. When some of the critical information is withheld, disastrous personal and organizational effects may result. When information is shared morale rises and productivity increases.

The same is true of a diocese or a parish. Through the circulation of information parishioners can make informed decisions, and live lives based on adequate and meaningful information. It is important that information is a goal and a result of effective leadership and change projects. Informed individuals create a stronger and more informed community.

3. *Transformation* is the result of caring. By caring for parishioners and parishes, both are transformed. Parishes affirm and call forth the charism of caring in individuals, i.e., they lead others to care for others. Most importantly, by their own example in caring for others parishes are able to transform parishioners into becoming more caring people. When parishioners feel empowered and encouraged to care for others, the mutual caring helps transform the parish into a more noble and more caring institution by the services it renders to everyone.

The questions that we must ask our parishes are:

• Is our parish community actually transforming the lives of its parishioners through the ministries it offers?

• How are we able to evaluate the quality and effectiveness of that transformation in the lives of parishioners in its ministries of worship, service, administration and education?

> Today's Catholics turn to their parish as participants and leaders, using it as an outlet for their talents. The parish is no longer a haven from the outside community, it is a vehicle for relating to and transforming that community.[5]

4. *Re-formation* is the fourth result. By respecting the evolving and changing needs of people in different cultures, geographic areas and parishes, reformation through structural reorganization and spiritual revitalization may be called for. Parishes can use a synergistic plan of action to maintain, develop or change any aspects of the four parish community ministries: Worshiping, Servicing, Administering and Educating.

> Christ summons the Church, as she goes her pilgrim way, to that continual reformation of which she always has need . . .[6]

9

A Parish Plan of Action:
5 Reorganization Phases

How do parish leaders actually produce "miraculous results?" That is, how do they form community, inform it, transform it and reform it. They need a plan of action.

You and I can cite examples of individuals who were great persons, who possessed fundamental values and had dreams for fulfilling the needs of individuals and institutions. However, when they were elected or selected to positions of leadership their potential never materialized. Dreams were not transformed into realities. Values did not influence important decisions. Their charisms remained inert potentialities. They were still "good persons." But, they did not become effective leaders. They were not able to form a sense of community, nor to transform the lives of people, nor to inform them coherently, nor to re-form what needed reformed.

What happens to such individual leaders? They are good *persons*. They possess specific *values*. They have *dreams* and possess some *power*. They want to produce *results*. These five conceptual elements of the paradigm exist in an internal, inherent and potential state. As such they are primal sources that can give birth to leadership and from which its effects proceed.

Perhaps an analogy may give some insights into the problem of unfulfilled leadership. Drops of water form a spring. This is the primal source from which streams of water begin to flow. The streams of water can dry up or become ponds, lakes, creeks and rivers. Dams and water canals can be built to direct the flow of water for irrigation and transportation, and to produce and transmit power for electricity, heat, air-conditioning and light.

In a similar way, the elements of our Leadership Paradigm form a primal source which gives birth to individual and corporate leadership and from which leadership activity flows to impact individual parishioners and entire parishes. This pool of leadership talent must not remain insipid, inert pools of potential energy. Leadership potential must be transformed into kinetic, powerful channels of leadership activity which produces powerful results.

One way of transforming that potential into real action is to develop and implement a Plan of Action. An Action Plan can help channel and transmit leaders' dreams and values into a powerful, kinetic source of enlightenment and positive movement for the Church.

An Action Plan emphasizes interdependence and synergy. The success of the parish plan depends upon everyone working together. It belongs to "everyone" who has a stake in the enterprise and "everyone" who will be directly affected by the implementation of the plan.

Together, parishioners envision a dream. Together, they synergize their complementary charisms in a team approach. In a spirit of complementarity they respect each other's values and share the power they have to cause good things to happen for the parish community.

In our proposed Parish Plan of Action we have developed five phases of action which can lead to successful parish revitalization and reorganization. The five phases are:

   I.   1. Synergizing: team building (organizing)

          2. Empowering: sharing power (mobilizing)

  II.   Enspiriting: clarifying parish values

 III.   Envisioning: developing shared parish dreams

 IV.   Enacting: developing and implementing a plan

  V.   Monitoring: supervising people and evaluating progress

A *Plan of Action* is the sixth conceptual element of the Leadership Paradigm. According to our typological approach, there are *four types* of plans. Parishes might integrate all four types into one comprehensive plan of action. Or, at times, one type of plan may be preferable and needed for a specific situation.

1. A Plan of Action can be EFFICIENT when parish leaders rely on their authority to organize and mobilize their followers and workers. They insist that they must be competent, and that they have mastered specific predetermined skills, concepts and attitudes. They require them to do the daily job in a competent manner. Their skills of day-to-day efficient management, short-range planning, organizing, coordinating and scheduling bring order and consistency to the project or task at hand.

2. A Plan of Action can be EFFECTIVE when parish leaders are both leaders and servants. As leaders they determine what is important and of value for others in the Church. As servants they are able to locate financial resources, human and material resources, and use them in practical, concrete ways to serve the needs of people. They organize and mobilize their parishioners with a plan which is usually short-range and focuses on serving all needy people who could benefit from the charity of the Church which the servant-leader serves and leads.

3. A Plan of Action can be AFFECTIVE when parish leaders are community-leaders. They organize and mobilize their followers by encouraging them to develop informal plans of action based on interpersonal approaches. The purpose of the plan is to create a harmonious community. The plan which stresses interpersonal relationships attempts to create the right climate for mutual responsibility. This plan emphasizes tightly-structured values in a loosely-structured system.

4. A Plan of Action can be CREATIVE when parish leaders are prophet-leaders. They organize and mobilize their followers when they develop long-range, comprehensive plans focusing on effective action which could change environmen-

tal circumstances and institutional structures. They scrutinize the signs of the times, interpret them and develop creative and ingenious plans for effective reform and renewal.

Plan of Action for Parish Reorganization

PHASES: QUESTIONS TO BE ANSWERED IN EACH PHASE:

I.	1. SYNERGIZING:	*Who* are the people who should be on our leadership-team? *What* are our complementary charisms?
	2. EMPOWERING:	*How* can we share power with people in order to mobilize them for action?
II.	ENSPIRITING:	*What* are the priority values of our parish? *Why* are we doing this?
III.	ENVISIONING:	*What* are our dreams? *What* is the parish mission?
IV.	ENACTING:	*How* do we develop and implement our plans?
V.	MONITORING:	*How* do we supervise people and evaluate progress?

Phase I: Synergizing and Empowering

I. 1. Synergizing

To synergize is to organize. To empower is to mobilize. A typological approach, however, suggests that individual leaders have preferred ways of organizing and mobilizing their followers. Usually, leaders can be successful when they incorporate all four types of plans into one comprehensive action plan. That is, the successful plan is one that is efficient, effective, affective and creative. It is also successful when parish leaders organize a leadership team by coordinating the charisms of individuals they select to be team members. Synergizing is based on five organizational principles and five implementation procedures.

A. The Five Principles of Synergizing

1) *the principle of grace building on nature:*

> Each member of the team must be a healthy person; a person of sound mind and spirit who is capable of working, and of working together with others. Actual grace can build more productively on a sound person with integrity (wholeness).

2) *the principle of complementary relationships:*

> The best teamwork is usually done by people who differ on one or two (personality-type) preferences only. This much difference is useful, and the two or three preferences they have in common help them to understand each other and communicate.[1]

3) *the principle of supportive relationships:*

> The leadership and other processes of the organization must be such as to ensure a maximum probability that in all interactions and all relationships with the organization each member will, in the light of his background, values, and expectations, view the experience as supportive and one which builds and maintains his sense of personal worth and importance.[2]

4) *the principle of overlapping relationships:*

> . . . leaders will make full use of the potential capacities of their human resources only when each person in an organization is a member of one or more effectively functioning work groups . . . .[3]

5) *the principle of interlinking relationships:*

> . . . an organization will function best when its personnel function not as individuals but as members of highly effective work groups with high performance goals. Consequently, (leaders) should deliberately endeavor to build these effective groups, linking them into an over-all organization by means of people who hold over-lapping group membership. The superior in one group is a subordinate in the next group, and so on through

the organization. If the work groups at each hierarchical level are well knit and effective, the linking process will be accomplished well. Staff as well as line should be characterized by this pattern of operation.[4]

Leaders organize their followers based on the above five principles in order to finish the task, to turn dreams into realities, to maintain the status quo, to orchestrate change, to build personal relationships, to develop a sense of community, to solve problems, to meet challenges, to think, to feel, to cause good things to happen to people.

Who can do all of these things? People who work together in unified action can do all of these things, and more! Leaders can build teams which work in synergy by using the following five procedures:

B. The Five Procedures for Synergizing

1) Leaders help team members understand how their needs, values, dreams, etc. differ from person to person by applying the Leadership Paradigm and its individual components to every person on the team. In other words, leaders are able to recognize and point out the characteristics of each team member's Spirit, Power, Vision, Personality-type, and the types of results they prefer.

2) Leaders help team members understand their strengths and weaknesses. (See Apendix A.) Team members can discuss what they do best as a team, and what they might not do so well. They should add to the team those persons who possess charisms that are still needed and not currently represented on the team.

3) Leaders help team members determine the "majority type" and "minority type" in the group. The most recurring personality-type among team members will have a major influence on the character and actions of the team. The personality-type that is in the minority will probably have a minor effect on the group's character and actions. Team members should be sensitive to this possible situation.

4) Leaders help team members gain a wholesome respect for the important opposite qualities that others possess. There is a need within the team

to identify the complementarity of other types in order to build a well-balanced, fully functioning team.

5) Leaders encourage team members to collaborate on specific tasks by helping them understand the mutual usefulness of similar and opposite types. They can help team members identify their strengths and weaknesses based on the four basic personality-types. They can use this information to help them work together in any process that will be needed in forming and implementing the action plan. (See pp. 43-45, "The Four Basic Personality Types.")

This approach is useful for team building. However, it is not fool-proof. Nevertheless, it is one process which helps leaders look at the talents and charisms that each member brings to the leadership team. The leader can explain to each member, individually and in the presence of the entire group, what charisms the leader believes each member brings to the team. The leader can illustrate how they can complement each other in a proposed synergistic leadership-team effort.

When leaders recognize and acknowledge the charisms and talents of others, they begin to empower them. They make them feel good about themselves. They ennoble other persons by telling them that they are persons who can act nobly when they use their charisms in service to others in the Church and parish community. They help the Church and parish community become a more noble and more caring institution. They themselves become more noble.

I.2. Empowering

The word, empowerment, means that power is being shared purposely with someone else. When people are being given a share in power, they no longer feel powerless. Rather, they feel that they have some control over their lives because they are being asked to help make decisions about those issues in their lives that directly affect them. As we have already written, the shared-power that we are talking about is the power of love. Love is knowing, caring, respecting and responding. When parish leaders use the "miracle" of empowering their parishioners, they are implementing the following four procedures:

A. *Leaders acknowledge each person in the parish by name.*

They know their people and they recognize their talents and charisms. They communicate the feeling to them that they are significant and valuable. Calling followers by name gives them a sense of importance and a certain degree of acceptance. (The bigness of huge parishes is an obvious obstacle to the empowerment process.) Nevertheless, when individual persons are called by name and are invited to share their dreams and use their charisms and to help make decisions for the good of the Church, individuals are affirmed and the Church will benefit.

B. *Leaders establish a feeling of connectedness with people.*

This is accomplished when leaders and other parishioners genuinely care for one another. Leaders begin to convey that special feeling when they exhibit a willingness to be open about themselves. They do not hide their feelings and thoughts, dreams and doubts, strengths and weaknesses. Their own self-disclosure enables followers to do the same. It encourages them to "tell their stories," to share and begin to care.

C. *Leaders form reciprocal relationships which are necessary in parishes.*

Synergy and interdependence are the keystones. People must be willing to give and receive help. Parish leaders must be willing to listen to the "stories" and dreams of others. Realizing that others have talents and charisms, leaders provide opportunities for people to develop and use them productively. Empowering-leaders invite people formally and informally to share, grow and mutually support one another. They can form personal and professional support groups, prayer groups, quality circles, smaller communities within the large parish based on mutual interests and needs, think tanks, feeling tanks and other similar groups. Parish leaders invite others to do things for themselves. They provide them with the financial and technical expertise they need to be successful. Leaders create decision-making opportunities for them.

D. *Leaders invite others to help.*

Parish leaders must reach out to others and ask them to participate in the shared enterprise of the parish. "Ask not what your country can do for you, but what you can do for your country," said John F. Kennedy. People feel valuable, capable and worthwhile when they are asked to do something for other people, and when they are invited to work in synergy with others. We feel good about ourselves when we are able to use our knowledge, expertise and experience to help others do the things that we value. In addition, a negative "welfare mentality" is avoided because people can give as well as receive.

When leaders take these four steps they are empowering others to share in the satisfaction of having made decisions for the parish's successes and achievements. It means that others are learning leadership skills and processes. Trust, commitment and self esteem increase. More people feel more satisfied. They feel confident that their contributions in successful ventures will encourage their leaders to ask them again to share their talents. Tasks are completed and personal relationships evolve to form a community spirit. Not only are individuals empowered, but the entire parish is empowered to move forward.

A parish leadership-team is organized through the process of synergizing and they are mobilized through the process of empowerment.

Phase II: Enspiriting

When parish leaders feel a need to reorganize their parish and revitalize the communal life of the parish and the individual lives of parishioners, they can use the process of enspiriting to help people get in touch with their own values and the values the parish emphasizes through its ministries. In other words, enspiriting is intended to help people discover what is important to the parish collectively and individually. Consequently, we have developed three different procedures to help parish leaders get in touch with what parishioners think and feel about their parish: (A) A Parish Survey, (B) A Parish In-Depth Self-Study, (C) A Parish Coat of Arms.

A. A PARISH SURVEY

A Parish Survey is a questionnaire which can be completed by the entire parish or by a random sample of parishioners. The Parish Survey has three sections. Section I solicits personal information about the respondent while seeking anonymity. Section II asks the respondent to address essential elements of the parish in five general areas of parish life: Community (questions 1 - 8); Worship & Prayer (questions 9 - 18); Education (questions 19 - 22); Service (questions 23 - 26); Administration (questions 27 - 34).

The results of the Parish Survey could be shared with all parishioners. And, then, a parish leadership-team could conduct an "In-Depth Parish Self-Study" in order to discuss more fully how well each element exists in the parish. Parish "Town Hall Meetings" could be conducted to communicate those findings. Parish leaders would invite all parishioners to add their perceptions, thoughts and feelings about their parish.

Parish Survey

SECTION I:

Please give us some information about yourself. Do not identify yourself by name. Circle only one letter for each item.

I AM:

1. (a) female (b) male

2. (a) a lay person
   (b) a diocesan priest or deacon
   (c) a religious priest or deacon
   (d) a religious sister or brother

3. (a) a pastor
   (b) a parochial vicar (assistant pastor)
   (c) a permanent deacon
   (d) a member of the parish staff
   (e) a member of parish council
   (f) a parishioner

4. (a) single
   (b) married
   (c) widowed
   (d) separated
   (e) divorced

5. (a) 16 - 25 years old
    (b) 26 - 40 years old
    (c) 41 - 55 years old
    (d) 56 - 70 years old
    (e) 71 and over.

6. (a) White
    (b) Black
    (c) Oriental
    (d) Hispanic
    (e) Other

7. (a) very active in my parish
    (b) somewhat active in my parish
    (c) I attend Mass but I am not active in my parish
    (d) not active at all in my parish

8. (a) very attached to my parish
    (b) somewhat attached to my parish
    (c) not at all attached to my parish
    (d) not sure how I feel about my parish

SECTION II: MY PERCEPTIONS ABOUT PARISH LIFE

34 elements of parish life are listed below. They may be found in any parish in the United States.

First, rate how *important* each element is to you by circling *one* of the following on the *left* side of the page:

VI = Very Important; I = Important; NI = Not Important.

Then, rate *how well* each element exists *in your parish* (the *quality*) by circling *one* of the following on the *right* side of the page:

G=Good; F=Fair; P=Poor; N=Does Not Exist in My Parish; DK = Don't Know.

IMPORTANCE	PARISH ELEMENTS	QUALITY
	MY PARISH:	
1. VI I NI	is a caring community.	G F P N DK
2. VI I NI	welcomes people into the parish.	G F P N DK
3. VI I NI	calls active Catholics to a deeper faith.	G F P N DK
4. VI I NI	invites fallen-away Catholics back to the Church.	G F P N DK
5. VI I NI	reaches out to people not active in any Church.	G F P N DK
6. VI I NI	participates in local ecumenical activities.	G F P N DK
7. VI I NI	reaches out to the youth of the parish.	G F P N DK
8. VI I NI	maintains an ethnic/racial heritage.	G F P N DK
9. VI I NI	provides Mass for Sundays and Holy Days.	G F P N DK
10. VI I NI	provides Mass every day.	G F P N DK
11. VI I NI	provides other worship services (e.g., novenas, penance services, anointing services, etc.)	G F P N DK
12. VI I NI	encourages people to participate in Mass.	G F P N DK
13. VI I NI	invites parishioners to serve as lectors, cantors, ushers, Eucharistic ministers, altar servers, etc.	G F P N DK

14. VI I NI   provides the Sacrament of Confession/Reconciliation
               weekly at regularly scheduled times.   G F P N DK

15. VI I NI   emphasizes personal holiness and religious growth.   G F P N DK

16. VI I NI   prepares people to receive the sacraments.   G F P N DK

17. VI I NI   provides for sacramental needs of sick and shut- ins.   G F P N DK

18. VI I NI   makes the gospel relevant by applying it to the lives
               of parishioners through the homily.   G F P N DK

19. VI I NI   provides education through the parish/regional/merged
               elementary school.   G F P N DK

20. VI I NI   provides CCD for elementary school students.   G F P N DK

21. VI I NI   provides CCD for high school students.   G F P N DK

22. VI I NI   provides opportunities for adults to grow in their knowledge
               of the faith.   G F P N DK

23. VI I NI   provides help for those in need, when it can.   G F P N DK

24. VI I NI   sponsors or supports efforts such as AA, food banks, blood
               drives, etc.   G F P N DK

25. VI I NI   assists in obtaining help for those in need when the parish
               itself cannot provide help.   G F P N DK

26. VI I NI   reaches out to parishioners with special needs (e.g. elderly,
               single parents, unemployed, etc.)   G F P N DK

27. VI I NI   invites people to share the responsibility of leading   G F P N DK
               the parish.

28. VI I NI   supports its leaders (priests/staff/parish council).   G F P N DK

29. VI I NI   has sufficient staff.   G F P N DK

30. VI I NI   provides periodic financial reports to parishioners.   G F P N DK

31. VI I NI   maintains its property and buildings.   G F P N DK

32. VI I NI   is financially secure.   G F P N DK

33. VI I NI   is supported primarily by Offertory contributions.   G F P N DK

34. VI I NI   has adequate facilities.   G F P N DK

SECTION III: ATTITUDES ABOUT THE FUTURE

Imagine that you lived in an area where there were four Catholic parishes with a total of five priests, and it becomes certain that only three priests will be available in the very near future.

1. What would you recommend be done for the spiritual vitality of the people in these four parishes: (Circle One.)

    (a) Keep all four parishes open as they are.
    (b) Keep all four parishes open, but make creative administrative changes.
    (c) Close one or more of the parishes.
    (d) Merge all of the parishes together.
    (e) I don't know.

2. Who, in your opinion, should be involved in deciding what should be done? (Circle One.)

    (a) The Bishop alone.
    (b) The Bishop with the pastors of the four parishes.
    (c) The Bishop, the pastors, and the parish councils.
    (d) The Bishop, the pastors, the parish councils, and all the parishioners of the four parishes.

B. AN IN-DEPTH PARISH SELF-STUDY GUIDEBOOK

This "Guidebook" is both a book and a guide. It is a "book" which contains many ideas about parish life. The ideas describe the same five general areas of parish life which are found in the "Parish Survey." However, the ideas are described in much more detail. They are called "Parish Vitality Indicators" because they indicate what elements can give vitality to a parish.

It is a "guide" because the "Parish Vitality Indicators" systematically escort the members of the Parish Leadership Team (Task Force) through a study of many important elements of parish life. It guides the Task Force in considering what should remain the same and what changes should be made. The Guidebook can guide the parish to structural reorganization and spiritual revitalization.

A Parish Task Force is a group of parish leaders representing the parish in working through the In-Depth Parish Self-Study. It is their responsibility to determine whether the elements of parish vitality exist in their parish and how much improvement might be needed.

A Parish Task-Force may choose one of several different approaches in completing the In-Depth Parish Self-Study:

1. The Pastor and staff may decide that 24 - 30 people should be on the Parish Task Force. Four or five members of the Task Force may comprise five different work groups, one for each of the five areas of parish vitality. Each work group can bring its findings to the whole group for review and final evaluation.

2. A parish may prefer a smaller Task Force which has 10 -14 members. In this case, the whole Task Force could work through each of the five areas of parish vitality. This process may require more time. However, everyone on the Task Force would be involved in the total In-Depth Study.

In the Diocese of Pittsburgh in November, 1989, the above Parish Survey was mailed to 50,000 Catholics. 42,000 of those surveys were mailed to a random sample of Catholics in 309 parishes in the six counties of Southwestern Pennsylvania which constitute the Diocese of Pittsburgh. The remaining 8,000 surveys were mailed to the parish clergy, parish staff and parish council members.

The response was tremendous. 45% of the random sample and 75% of the clergy, staff and parish council members returned their surveys. The surveys were electronically scored and tabulated by a Scantron machine and computer. The results were tabulated according to individual parish, deanery, and diocese, and according to the three groupings of random sample, clergy and staff, and parish council of each parish.

The results were communicated by the local secular media, by the *Pittsburgh Catholic* newspaper, in church bulletins and in every parish through "town hall meetings" where all parishioners were invited to listen and respond to the results.

In Pittsburgh the pastor and staff were asked to select two parish co-directors for the parish self-study process. They were trained in the process and taught the needed skills to facilitate the in-depth self-study and town hall meetings at a series of workshops which were scheduled in various locations and at different times. They, with their pastors, were responsible for choosing a Parish Task Force which would evaluate parish life by using this In-Depth Parish Self-Study Guidebook.

Pastors were invited to the workshops. Separate workshops were scheduled for all of the clergy. In our opinion, this on-going leadership development for laity and clergy would be the key to success. At this time, we would like to remind the reader about our comments in the Introduction of this book, i.e., *organization development and leadership development are the two basic ingredients of successful planned change.*

These are the instructions that we provided for the two parish directors in every parish and for the pastors so that they would be able to *lead* their parish task force through the in-depth self-study.

General Instructions

The "Indicators of Parish Vitality" are divided into five general categories. Each category is then divided into three or four areas (see below).

1. Begin by reading the introductory remarks for the category which you will be discussing and rating.

2. Review the question for the specific area which you will be rating.

3. Using the consensus process described on pages 118-119, rate each indicator of parish vitality by entering the appropriate rating number on the line opposite that indicator (see "Rating Scale," page 117).

4. Give a reason for your rating, e.g., by supplying a brief description or example to support and/or clarify your evaluation.

5. After you have completed each specific rating, rate your parish's *overall* effort for each area.

6. After each category (i.e, Community, Worship, Service, Education and Administration), identify the greatest strength of the parish in that category and the area most in need of improvement within that category.

7. Proceed in the same way for each category, each area within the categories, and for each indicator of vitality within each area.

8. When every category, area and indicator have been evaluated, record the overall results on the summary sheet.

Category	Area
I. Community:	A. Welcoming B. Evangelization C. Diversity of Talents D. Distinctive Community
II. Worship and Prayer:	A. Weekend Liturgies B. Liturgical Year C. Sacraments
III. Service:	A. Parish Community B. Local Community C. Global Community
IV. Education	A. Youth B. Adults C. Variety of Needs
V. Administration:	A. Stewardship B. Shared Responsibility C. Interdependence

The Rating Scale for Each Indicator of the In-Depth Self-Study

1 = The parish's effort in this area is
OUTSTANDING. The work and results
are of the highest quality.

No significant
improvement or
development is
required.

2 = The parish's effort in this area is
VERY GOOD. The work and results
are often of the highest quality.

3 = The parish's effort in this area is
GOOD. The work and results are
above average.

Little significant
improvement or
development is
required.

4 = The parish's effort in this area is
SATISFACTORY*. The work and
results are at an acceptable level.

5 = The parish's effort in this area is
FAIR. The work and results are at
times below what is acceptable.

Some significant
improvement or
development is
required.

6 = The parish's effort in this area is
POOR. The work and results are
often below minimum expectation.

7 = The parish's effort in this area is
EXTREMELY POOR. The work and
results are totally unacceptable.

Much significant
improvement or
development is
required.

8 = This indicator is *NOT APPLICABLE.*

(Explain why this
indicator is "not
applicable.")

---

*"Satisfactory" means that the effort of the parish is in accord with:
   1) the teachings of the universal Church;
   2) the applicable guidelines of the Diocese;
   3) the needs of the people who belong *OR* could belong to this parish.

A PROCESS FOR RATING EACH INDICATOR: CONSENSUS

TASK #1: Begin by becoming familiar with the category, area, and specific indicator which you will be discussing.

Step 1.1: Read the appropriate material in the manual and invite task force members to ask any questions which could clarify what the indicator means.

Step 1.2: Briefly share with group members information about your parish's activities which relate to this indicator. You might want to ask people who are knowledgeable in the area you are discussing (e.g., school principal, Finance Council member, etc.) to prepare a brief written or oral report for the Task Force.

TASK #2: *Without discussion,* solicit group members' initial rating of the indicator under review.

Step 2.1: Draw a horizontal line across a chalkboard, newsprint, or overhead transparency, as below.

1	2	3	4	5	6	7	8

Step 2.2: Without discussion, ask each group member individually to rate the indicator from "1" to "8" (see Rating Scale").
Place an "X" under the number which represents their rating.

Step 2.3: Next, ask each group member to give a reason for their rating, e.g., by supplying a brief description or example to support and/or clarify his/her evaluation. Under the "X" which represents that person's opinion, write a word or two to summarize their reason for choosing that rating.

TASK #3: Agree on one number which indicates the group's consensus about the rating for each indicator.

Step 3.1: If group members are pretty much in agreement about the rating number, circle the rating number which indicates consensus, and move on to the next indicator.

Step 3.2:   If there is a spread of opinion among group members about the rating number, ask if any member wants to change his or her opinion after hearing the ratings and reasons from other group members. If, as a result of such changes, group members are pretty much in agreement, circle the rating number which indicates consensus, and move on to the next indicator.

Step 3.3:   If Step 3.2 does not lead to consensus, then invite the group to identify more fully the reasons (supporting evidence) for one rating over another. Keep track on the chalkboard, news-print, or overhead transparency of all the reasons given. After the group has identified as many reasons as they can for the various ratings, repeat Step 2.2 to determine if the group has arrived at consensus. If the group is now in agreement, circle the rating number which indicates consensus, and move on to the next indicator.

Step 3.4:   If, and only if, consensus cannot be reached within a reasonable amount of time, then record a majority and a minority report, and move on to the next indicator.

Indicator of Parish Vitality

I. THE PARISH IS A COMMUNITY.

This area of parish vitality relates to a parish's efforts to build a sense of community by including all members actively in the parish, by reaching out to the fallen-away and to those in the local community who do not belong to any Church, and by the parish's need to maintain special traditions and practices.

A. How would you describe the parish's effort to *welcome* all of its members into the life of the parish?

INDICATOR	RATING	REASON
1. The parish has an organized welcome program for new members.	_____	
2. Handicapped members are involved in every aspect of parish life according to their abilities.	_____	
3. The elderly are involved in publicly visible roles in the parish.	_____	
4. Adolescents and young adults are actively involved in the parish.	_____	
5. Persons of all races are welcome to participate fully in the life and ministry of the parish.	_____	
6. The size of the parish (number of parishioners) helps build a sense of community.	_____	
7. The size of the parish is conducive for sponsoring needed programs and activities for parishioners.	_____	

OVERALL EVALUATION OF PARISH AS A WELCOMING
COMMUNITY (Circle One)

1	2	3	4	5	6	7	8
NO IMPROVEMENT NEEDED		LITTLE IMPROVEMENT NEEDED		SOME IMPROVEMENT NEEDED		MUCH IMPROVEMENT NEEDED	

B. How would you describe the parish's efforts in *evangelization*?

INDICATOR	RATING	REASON
1. The parish reaches out to fallen-away Catholics.	_____	
2. The parish reaches out to people not participating in any Church.	_____	
3. The parish sponsors formal "come home" or other evangelization programs.	_____	
4. The parish has a door-to-door parish census	_____	

OVERALL EVALUATION OF PARISH EVANGELIZATION
(Circle One)

1	2	3	4	5	6	7	8
NO IMPROVEMENT NEEDED		LITTLE IMPROVEMENT NEEDED		SOME IMPROVEMENT NEEDED		MUCH IMPROVEMENT NEEDED	

C. How would you describe the parish's ability to recognize the *diversity of talents and needs* of its people?

INDICATOR   RATING   REASON

1. The parish consistently
   identifies and uses the talents   _____
   of parishioners.
2. Parish organizations invite people
   to participate in a variety of   _____
   activities.
3. Parishioners are supported in changing   _____
   their parish involvements as they grow
   older or develop new interests.
4. The parish is able to identify the   _____
   changing needs of parishioners.
5. Parishioners are encouraged to use   _____
   their talents for the good of the parish.

OVERALL EVALUATION OF PARISH RECOGNITION OF
DIVERSITY OF TALENTS AND NEEDS. (Circle One)

1	2	3	4	5	6	7	8
NO IMPROVEMENT NEEDED		LITTLE IMPROVEMENT NEEDED		SOME IMPROVEMENT NEEDED		MUCH IMPROVEMENT NEEDED	

D. How would you describe the parish as a *distinctive community*? That is, every parish is distinctive because it has special qualities, traditions, and/or practices that have evolved over the years. The population of every parish as it exists today also represents a distinctive blend of people, needs and talents.

INDICATOR   RATING   REASON

1. There is a need for non-English use in homilies, bulletins, hymns, group meetings and Reconciliation. _____

2. There is a desire for observances of specific feasts and practices related to ethnic traditions. _____

3. There is a level of membership specifically affiliated with the parish because of its ethnic roots. _____

4. There is a frequency and participation in devotions to saints, patrons of significance to the parish. _____

5. There is a frequency and participation in traditionally held parish social programs. _____

6. Strong bonds exist between the parish and a particular religious community. _____

7. The parish demonstrates respect for the various ethnic/racial backgrounds of its parishioners. _____

OVERALL EVALUATION OF A DISTINCTIVE PARISH COMMUNITY (Please Note: In this evaluation, we are *not* asking you to determine how much improvement is needed. Rather, we are asking *how significant* these elements are for the vitality of your parish.)

1	2	3	4	5	6	7	8
NOT SIGNIFICANT		MINIMALLY SIGNIFICANT		SOMEWHAT SIGNIFICANT		VERY SIGNIFICANT	

The parish's greatest strength as a Community is . . .

_____

_____

_____

_____

The area of the parish as a Community which needs the most improvement is . . .

_____

_____

_____

_____

II. THE PARISH IS A WORSHIPPING AND PRAYING COMMUNITY.
This indicator of parish vitality relates to liturgy, sacraments, renewal efforts, seasonal worship, devotions, prayer and other opportunies provided by the parish.

A. How would you describe *weekend liturgies*?

INDICATOR	RATING	REASON
1. Congregation is actively involved in the liturgy: e.g., join in prayer response, men & women are trained and active as lectors, eucharistic ministers, greeters, etc.	_____	
2. All approved liturgical roles open to both men and women.	_____	
3. Music is an important part of the weekend Masses: choir, congregational singing, cantors, etc.	_____	
4. The church environment is conducive for meaningful liturgy (e.g., flowers, decorations, adequate PA system, clean church, etc.	_____	
5. The number of weekend Masses is based on the number of parishioners, priests and needs of both.	_____	
6. Communion is offered under both species of bread and wine.	_____	
7. Homilies are relevant to the needs and cares of people.	_____	

OVERALL EVALUATION OF PARISH WEEKEND LITURGIES
(Circle One)

1	2	3	4	5	6	7	8
NO IMPROVEMENT NEEDED		LITTLE IMPROVEMENT NEEDED		SOME IMPROVEMENT NEEDED		MUCH IMPROVEMENT NEEDED	

B. How would you describe other worship practices and opportunties to pray throughout the *liturgical year*?

INDICATOR	RATING	REASON
1. During Advent and Lent special liturgical practices are scheduled.	_____	
2. Special Feast Days are celebrated through the year.	_____	
3. Prayer groups, novenas, days of recollection, missions, and faith sharing opportunities are offered.	_____	
4. Formal renewal programs exist.	_____	
5. Special blessings and prayer services for new parents, anniversaries, vocations, etc., are offered.	_____	
6. Opportunities to worship together are provided for a variety of groups with common interests (e.g., family, teenagers, social organizations, etc.)	_____	
7. Weekday Masses are scheduled according to the needs of people and time constraints of priests.	_____	

OVERALL EVALUATION OF PARISH LITURGICAL YEAR SERVICES (Circle One)

1	2	3	4	5	6	7	8
	NO IMPROVEMENT NEEDED		LITTLE IMPROVEMENT NEEDED		SOME IMPROVEMENT NEEDED		MUCH IMPROVEMENT NEEDED

C. How would you describe parish participation in and provisions of *sacraments?*

INDICATORS   RATING   REASON

1. Shut-ins and ill are visited   _____
   with Eucharistic regularly.
2. RCIA is being implemented and   _____
   involves families and the entire
   community.
3. Penance services and reconciliation   _____
   are offered in both forms.
4. Baptisms, weddings and funerals are   _____
   community celebrations.
5. Anointing Services are offered on a   _____
   regular basis.

OVERALL EVALUATION OF PARISH SACRAMENTAL LIFE
(Circle One)

1	2	3	4	5	6	7	8
	NO IMPROVEMENT NEEDED		LITTLE IMPROVEMENT NEEDED		SOME IMPROVEMENT NEEDED		MUCH IMPROVEMENT NEEDED

The parish's greatest strength as a Worshipping Community is . . .

_____

_____

_____

_____

The area of the parish as a Worshipping Community which needs the most improvement is . . .

_____

_____

_____

_____

III. THE PARISH IS A COMMUNITY OF SERVICE.

This area of parish vitality includes serving the poor, the alienated, the elderly, families and other needy people in the community both in and beyond the parish. It is in this area of parish life that peace, justice, and advocacy for those in need are actively pursued.

A. How would you describe the degree to which the parish reaches out to its *own members* who are in need?

INDICATOR	RATING	REASON
1. The parish employs a parish social service minister.	_____	
2. The parish has support groups for those with special needs (e.g., newly married, single parents, elderly, bereaved, new parents, separated/divorced, unemployed, chemically dependent, etc.)	_____	
3. Parishioners respond when invited to volunteer for various parish service programs.	_____	
4. The parish is sensitive to the needs of families when it schedules ministries, programs and events.	_____	
5. Awareness of social issues is raised through homilies, formal discussions of encyclicals, pastoral letters, etc.	_____	

OVERALL EVALUATION OF PARISH SERVING ITS OWN MEMBERS (Circle One)

1	2	3	4	5	6	7	8
NO IMPROVEMENT NEEDED		LITTLE IMPROVEMENT NEEDED		SOME IMPROVEMENT NEEDED		MUCH IMPROVEMENT NEEDED	

B. How would you describe how well the parish participates in service to the *community beyond the parish?*

INDICATOR   RATING   REASON

1. The parish opens its facilities to _____
   community groups for meetings (e.g., AA).

2. The parish sponsors or supports _____
   local food banks, blood drives, resale
   shops, group homes, etc.

3. Parishioners are encouraged to be _____
   active in local school boards, community
   groups, service centers, hospitals, etc.

4. Parish participates in local _____
   ecumenical activities, (e.g., ministerial
   associations, seasonal services, etc.)

EVALUATION OF PARISH SERVICE TO LOCAL COMMUNITY.
(Circle One)

1	2	3	4	5	6	7	8
	NO IMPROVEMENT NEEDED		LITTLE IMPROVEMENT NEEDED		SOME IMPROVEMENT NEEDED		MUCH IMPROVEMENT NEEDED

C. How would you describe the extent of parish involvement in service to the larger world and/or in more *global issues?*

INDICATOR	RATING	REASON

1. Parishioners respond generously to diocesan appeals, clothing drives and other national efforts. _____

2. Parishioners participate in peace and justice activities, pro-life movement, voter registration drives, letter-writing campaigns, sponsoring missionaries, etc. _____

3. Parish uses offices of diocese which offer special services (e.g., legal help, peace and justice, world hunger, etc. _____

4. Parish calls attention to advocacy needs for state/federal legislation. _____

EVALUATION OF PARISH SERVICE TO GLOBAL WORLD. (Circle One)

1	2	3	4	5	6	7	8
NO IMPROVEMENT NEEDED		LITTLE IMPROVEMENT NEEDED		SOME IMPROVEMENT NEEDED		MUCH IMPROVEMENT NEEDED	

The parish's greatest strength as a Serving Community is . . .

_____

_____

_____

_____

The area of the parish as a Serving Community which needs the most improvement is . . .

_____

_____

_____

_____

IV. THE PARISH IS AN EDUCATING COMMUNITY.

This area of parish vitality includes all efforts to ensure that ongoing training in the faith and teachings of the Catholic Church are provided to parishioners of all ages depending on their needs.

A. How would you describe the parish's efforts to pass on the faith to its *youth* and strengthen it?

INDICATOR	RATING	REASON
1. The parish sponsors its own school or is a sponsor of a regional or merged elementary school.	_____	
2. The parish supports its students in other elementary schools with financial assistance and/or compliance with diocesan school subsidy policies.	_____	
3. The parish provides a full- or part-time, paid Director or Coordinator of Religious Education.	_____	
4. The parish offers viable CCD programs for families, children and youth.	_____	
5. The parish provides for and supports initial and on-going training for its catechists.	_____	
6. The parish encourages and supports parents as the primary religious educators of their children.	_____	

OVERALL EVALUATION OF PARISH EDUCATION OF YOUTH (Circle One)

1	2	3	4	5	6	7	8
NO IMPROVEMENT NEEDED		LITTLE IMPROVEMENT NEEDED		SOME IMPROVEMENT NEEDED		MUCH IMPROVEMENT NEEDED	

B. How would you describe the parish's effort to strengthen the faith and provide education to parish *adults*?

INDICATORS   RATING   REASON

1. The parish offers a variety of adult   _____
   education programs (e.g., Bible study,
   speakers, etc.)
2. The parish supports its lay ministers   _____
   and volunteers with inservice programs.
3. The parish makes books and   _____
   pamphlets related to the faith available.
4. The parish offers opportunities to   _____
   listen to and learn from parishioners of
   diverse family backgrounds about their
   faith.

EVALUATION OF PARISH EDUCATION OF ADULTS
(Circle One)

1	2	3	4	5	6	7	8
NO IMPROVEMENT NEEDED		LITTLE IMPROVEMENT NEEDED		SOME IMPROVEMENT NEEDED		MUCH IMPROVEMENT NEEDED	

C. How would you describe the parish's educational attempts to meet the *variety of educational needs* of different parishioners?

INDICATOR   RATING   REASON

1. The parish provides for peer   _____
   involvement in baptism and marriage
   preparation.
2. The parish provides occasional   _____
   educational programs in special need
   areas such as single parenting, divorce,
   caring for the elderly or handicapped, etc.
3. The parish arranges for sacramental   _____
   preparation and catechesis for parishioners
   with mental retardation and other disabilities.

EVALUATION OF PARISH TO MEET VARIETY OF EDUCATION-
AL NEEDS (Circle One)

1	2	3	4	5	6	7	8
NO IMPROVEMENT NEEDED		LITTLE IMPROVEMENT NEEDED		SOME IMPROVEMENT NEEDED		MUCH IMPROVEMENT NEEDED	

The parish's greatest strength as an Educating Community is . . .

_____

_____

_____

_____

The area of the parish as an Educating Community which needs the most improvement is . . .

_____

_____

_____

_____

V. THE PARISH IS AN ADMINISTERING COMMUNITY.
This area of parish vitality relates to the leadership, administration, management and decision-making processes of the parish, as well as to the relationship of the parish to the rest of the institutional Church.

A. How well does the parish incorporate principles of good *stewardship* in managing its financial resources?

INDICATOR	RATING	REASON
1. The parish staff are paid just wages.	_____	
2. The parish has operated in the black over each of the last several years and met its ordinary expenses in a timely fashion.	_____	
3. Parish operations are not overly dependent on special fund-raising activities such as fairs and bingo.	_____	
4. The parish is satisfied with the amount of money collected from weekend offertory contributions.	_____	
5. The parish works to retire any debt it has incurred and keeps up with interest payments on a timely basis.	_____	
6. The parish maintains its plant and facilities in good condition.	_____	
7. Parish facilities are adequate for our present and future needs, both liturgically and for other parish uses.	_____	

OVERALL EVALUATION OF PARISH STEWARDSHIP
(Circle One)

1	2	3	4	5	6	7	8
	NO IMPROVEMENT NEEDED		LITTLE IMPROVEMENT NEEDED		SOME IMPROVEMENT NEEDED		MUCH IMPROVEMENT NEEDED

B. How well does the Parish share *leadership and responsibility* with parishioners.

INDICATOR	RATING	REASON
1. The parish has an active Parish Council which regularly advises the pastor.	_____	
2. The parish has an active Finance council.	_____	
3. Parishioners and others exhibit an obvious respect and care for parish facilities and the physical plant.	_____	
4. Parishioners help care for and maintain parish grounds and facilities.	_____	
5. Parishioners assist in fund-raising activities.	_____	
6. Parishioners are given opportunities to share in leadership responsibilities by being empowered to use their skills and experiences for the good of the parish.	_____	

OVERALL EVALUATION OF SHARED PARISH LEADERSHIP AND RESPONSIBILITY
(Circle One)

1	2	3	4	5	6	7	8
NO IMPROVEMENT NEEDED		LITTLE IMPROVEMENT NEEDED		SOME IMPROVEMENT NEEDED		MUCH IMPROVEMENT NEEDED	

C. How would you describe the parish's efforts to cooperate
interdependently with other parishes and the diocese?

INDICATOR   RATING   REASON

1. The parish shares resources or   _____
   programs with other local parishes.
2. The parish participates in diocesan-   _____
   wide activities and groups (e.g., DCCW
   Holy Name, regional information meetings,
   conferences, etc.)
3. The parish contributes to deanery   _____
   and other regional discussions and activities.
4. The parish makes an effort to know and   _____
   comply with diocesan policy and guidelines
   affecting parish programs.

OVERALL EVALUATION OF PARISH INTERDEPENDENCE
WITH OTHER PARISHES AND WITH THE DIOCESE
(Circle One)

1	2	3	4	5	6	7	8

NO   LITTLE   SOME   MUCH
IMPROVEMENT   IMPROVEMENT   IMPROVEMENT   IMPROVEMENT
NEEDED   NEEDED   NEEDED   NEEDED

The parish's greatest strength as an Administering Community is . . .

_____

_____

_____

_____

The area of the parish as an Administering Community which needs the most improvement is . . .

_____

_____

_____

_____

SUMMARY SHEET FOR PARISH IN-DEPTH SELF-STUDY

PARISH: _____

ADDRESS: _____

INDICATORS OF
PARISH VITALITY   IMPROVEMENT NEEDED

	NONE		LITTLE		SOME		MUCH	

I. COMMUNITY

1. Welcoming	1	2	3	4	5	6	7	8
2. Evangelization	1	2	3	4	5	6	7	8
3. Diversity of Talents	1	2	3	4	5	6	7	8

SIGNIFICANCE

4. Distinctive Community	1	2	3	4	5	6	7	8

II. WORSHIP & PRAYER

1. Weekend Liturgies	1	2	3	4	5	6	7	8
2. Liturgical Year Services	1	2	3	4	5	6	7	8
3. Sacramental Life	1	2	3	4	5	6	7	8

III. SERVICE

1. Parish	1	2	3	4	5	6	7	8
2. Community	1	2	3	4	5	6	7	8
3. World	1	2	3	4	5	6	7	8

IV. EDUCATION

1. Youths	1	2	3	4	5	6	7	8
2. Adults	1	2	3	4	5	6	7	8
3. Variety of Needs	1	2	3	4	5	6	7	8

V. ADMINISTRATION

1. Stewardship	1	2	3	4	5	6	7	8
2. Shared Responsibility	1	2	3	4	5	6	7	8
3. Interdependence	1	2	3	4	5	6	7	8

STATISTICAL INDICATORS OF PARISH VITALITY

1. # of parishioners   _____

2. # of people attending Weekend Masses in Oct. 1989   _____

3. % of people attending Weekend Masses in Oct. 1989   _____

4. % of population change between 1980-1988   _____

5. # of Weekend Masses   _____

6. Average attendance at each Weekend Mass   _____

7. Seating capacity of church   _____

8. # of full-time priests assigned to parish   _____

9. Ratio of parishioners to parish priest(s)   _____

10. # of baptisms (1989)   _____

11. # of funerals (1989)   _____

12. # of marriages (1989)   _____

13. Annual regular offertory collection   _____

14. Average regular weekly offertory collection   _____

15. Parish savings   _____

16. Parish debt   _____

C. A Parish Coat of Arms

Parish leaders can clarify parish values by drawing a parish coat of arms. This process is designed to help the parish leadership-team explore the parish's most strongly held values. It also helps them to experience the importance of giving public testimony to the parish's basic beliefs. There is some risk-taking involved because everyone will be wearing their values out front on their heraldic shields.

Everyone on the leadership team is asked to draw a shield (see next page). The shield is divided into five sections. The first four sections will contain pictures or images. Only the fifth section will contain words. The facilitator or leader gives the following instructions:

A. In section 1 draw two pictures or images. One image should represent something the parish is good at; the other picture should represent something you would like the parish to be good at.

B. In section 2 draw a picture or image that represents the one value from which the parish should never budge. You feel very deeply about this value and the parish should never give it up.

C. Imagine that your parish could accomplish anything you wished, and that your parish would be successful at it. Draw a picture or image of that accomplishment in section 3.

D. In section 4 draw pictures or images of several values that you would like all people in your parish to believe in and strive for.

E. You can write words in section 5. Write five words which you *hope* non-parishioners would use to describe your parish.

Finally, in the top section of the shield that is marked "motto" write a word or a phrase that you think would accurately describe the basic values and mission of your parish.

"Parish Coat of Arms"

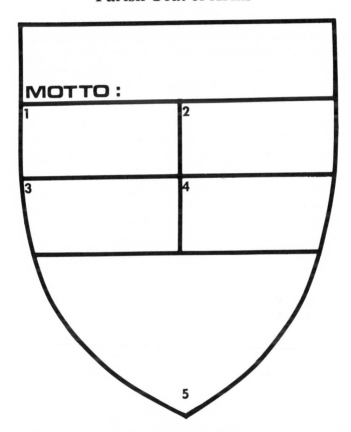

The motto and the values which have been expressed in drawing a "Parish Coat of Arms" can be incorporated in the Parish's Mission Statement as goals and objectives to be fulfilled by the parish. This exercise can help parish leaders begin to envision what their parish mission should be.

Phase III: Envisioning

A shared vision can point a parish to greatness. It can clarify the image and mission of the parish. It can help mobilize parishioners' energies and charisms based on their dreams and wishes. It is the leader's (e.g., pastor's, parish council member's) task to articulate clearly what the Vision is.

The envisioning process is a group effort. It begins with a group of individual persons who have a personal dream for the parish. The envisioning process is not so much concerned about "what *I* want" as it is with "what *we* want." For a parish it begins with an individual person's mental image of the ideal parish. Each person involved in the process contributes to the painting of a multi-faceted mental image. The huge challenge of the envisioning process is to paint a collective picture which everyone in the parish accepts and will work at. When the final Vision is a shared one, people tend to work together as a team. When parishioners become actively involved in shaping the Vision they become committed to making the Vision a reality. Their Vision can become so powerful that their picture of the future soon becomes a daily expression of their basic values and beliefs.

The success of the envisioning process depends on four attitudes that individuals need in order to bring about future change, and eight procedures that a leadership team can use to envision a dream for the parish.

A. *Attitudinal Approaches*

1. *We must be positive and creative* in approaching needed change. Creating a positive and creative image of how we want the parish to be is an effective approach in realizing necessary change. Even though negative forces and situations must be acknowledged, parishioners must use a positive developmental approach in imaging the future. A reactionary or negative approach is usually counterproductive for envisioning and developing parish change.

2. *We must proceed with hope.* Attitudes such as "If it ain't broke, don't fix it" and "things around here cannot change" contribute to a sense

of fatalism. Positive, creative proactive action plans arise out of the hope for something better in the future.

3. *We must proceed together.* Collaborative procedures, such as team work, synergizing, participative problem solving and shared decision making enable parishioners to share their charisms, values, dreams and power. Collaborative procedures help establish a climate conducive for successful envisioning.

4. *We must use a systems approach.* This type of approach helps people identify and deal with all of the significant challenges and problems in the system, rather than looking at individual, isolated problems. This approach allows individuals to look at several problems and challenges simultaneously in one big picture. In addition, in this approach:

> we discover that by relating seemingly divergent problems, we discover a root condition of greater importance, thus enabling the development of a vision that is more comprehensive and more compelling.[5]

Peter Drucker's comments on a systems approach are very insightful and relevant:

> One thing characterizes all genuine systems, whether they be mechanical like the control of a missile, biological like a tree, or social like the business enterprise: it is interdependence. The whole of a system is not necessarily improved if one particular function or part is improved or made more efficient. In fact, the system may well be damaged thereby, or even destroyed. In some cases the best way to strengthen the system may be to weaken a part—to make it less precise or less efficient. For what matters in any system is the performance of the whole.[6]

B. *Procedures for Envisioning*

1. The group facilitator invites the leader of the group to be an "envisioner."

2. As an envisioner, the leader is instructed to describe briefly what he or she likes about the current situation of the parish. Members of the group can ask only "clarifying questions," if they are uncertain about the in-

tended meaning. There is no discussion or debate. (The envisioner can use the "Parish Survey" or the "In-Depth Parish Self-Study" as a guide.)

3. After Step 1 is completed, the group facilitator invites the leader to describe briefly what he or she does not like about the parish. Again, there is no discussion or debate.

4. The group facilitator instructs everyone to listen carefully for significant phrases and key words that encapsulate the envisioner's description of the current situation. As they listen to the likes and dislikes of the leader, they draw pictures or images on their tablets that they feel describe what the envisioner is saying (the positive and the negative). Artistic talent is not needed nor necessarily desired.

5. The facilitator engages everyone in drawing a composite picture which includes all of the elements described by each member of the group.

6. As each member contributes drawings to the composite picture, they take turns interpreting their pictures to the large group.

7. A group recorder is responsible for writing on paper a list of specific significant ideas, values and beliefs that have been expressed.

8. The dreaming now begins. Now the facilitator asks all group members to dream about the ideal situation. Without thinking about any constraints which would prevent their dreams from becoming realities, each member privately draws images of his/her wishes and dreams on paper.

9. The facilitator engages everyone in drawing a Shared Vision of the ideal parish of the future. Each member individually approaches one large paper and draws images on it which they drew earlier on their individual pieces of paper. This group Vision represents their values, beliefs, tasks and mission of the parish.

10. The facilitator invites the leader of the group to draw the final big picture, the composite dream, the Parish Vision based on what he/she has seen and heard. All members of the group are invited to offer their input in developing this Shared Vision.

This envisioning process is another method for the Parish Task Force to discover what goals and objectives they have for their parish. The process can provide practical directions towards which the parish can move.

Phase IV: Enacting

A parish can move forward by reviewing both the dreams that have been shared through the envisioning process and the needs of people that have been discovered through the enspiriting process. Parish leaders can transform a shared vision and perceived needs into reality by writing clear parish goals, objectives and strategies, and a Parish Mission Statement.

A. *Writing Parish Goals*

Parish goals flow from the vision that parishioners have for the future parish community. A goal is a concise and clear statement of a general outcome or result which is intended by the parish. Each written parish goal would have the following characteristcs. A goal:

- is a general description of the intended result;

- is a concise description of the intended result;

- is a problem to be solved, challenge to be met or question to be answered;

- requires ownership;

- demands active participation by the task team;

- is realistic yet challenging;

- is attainable;

- is congruent with the mission and expectations of the Church.

The proper use of action verbs in goal statements is the key to successful goal writing. Each action verb is preceded by the preposition "to": to coordinate, to motivate, to participate, to share, to empower, to envision, to discuss, to appreciate, to renew, to reorganize, to revitalize, to develop, to form.

Here are several examples of parish goal statements:

- to form a caring, supportive parish community;

- to develop parish leaders;

- to revitalize the parish;

- to reorganize the parish;

- to motivate parishioners to grow spiritually;

- to share problem solving responsibilities with parishioners;

- to organize relevant and effective ministries to meet the needs of parishioners;

- to influence the lives of parishioners through meaningful and beautiful liturgies.

B. *Writing Parish Objectives*

A parish objective is a more specific and more clarified rendition of a goal statement. It too begins with the preposition "to" and is followed by an action verb. In addition, an objective intends to produce one measurable, quantifiable realistic result. A goal is more general and is not measurable.

Here are some examples of action words when writing objectives: to list, to identify, to design, to compare, to contrast, to evaluate, to disseminate, to approve, to measure.

Here are a few examples of parish objectives:

- to approve the budget;

- to list the names of the parish council members;

- to identify the scheduling problems that exist for the ushers at the Sunday Masses.

- to design a parish self-study instrument.

- to evaluate our parish mission statement and its objectives.

C. *Writing Strategies*

Strategies are the specific steps agreed to and listed by a parish leadership team in order to attain the objective and fulfill the goal. The strategies should be written in such a way that they answer the following questions:

- Who does what . . . , . . . and by when?

- What is the time line?

- What resources are needed? (i.e., financial, material resources, plus human resources as organized in a variety of parish ministries.)

- What is our theme, logo or motto?

- How will we evaluate our progress?

- How will we supervise the people who are responsible for implementing this project?

- How will we evaluate the final outcome or product?

- What is the rationale for trying to achieve this objective? In other words, why is this important to anyone?

- Have we considered all of the facts for the plan of action?

- Have we considered all of the relevant possibilities?

- Is the plan a logical one?

- How will the plan affect people?

- Do we have an effective Public Relations system to communicate our message and our mission?

D. *Writing a Parish Mission Statement*

In their pastoral letter, *A Shepherd's Care,* the bishops of the United States suggested that every parish should write a parish mission statement to give meaning, purpose and direction to the mission of the parish. A parish's mission statement or philosophy establishes the ideals or goals to which the parish subscribes. The statement of objectives identifies observable ways by which the philosophy is implemented. The objectives specify ideals (Vision and Spirit) which have been attained, are currently being attained, or are still a Vision to be realized. Prioritized goals and objectives are those ideals of such importance that they become a commitment of every parish ministry.

A parish may have one or more dreams that it would like to realize (Vision). It may have certain gospel values (Spirit) that it wants to pass on to people. Its Power of love may emphasize the need to care for the homeless in the inner city where the parish is located. Or, it may want to stress the need to inform people in their suburban parish through adult religious education. The Vision becomes concrete when the parish sees Results. Parish mission statements may differ from parish to parish, with the primary mission being always the same: to build the Kingdom of God (according to Vatican Council II).

Through the envisioning process, the shared dreams of the parish are listed. Through the exercises on writing goals, objectives and strategies, the group responsible for writing the statement should have all of the needed information. The parish philosophy answers the questions: who are we, what do we want to accomplish, and why do we want to do this?

Phase V: Monitoring

Monitoring procedures are mechanisms for measuring the progress and performance of the individual (supervision) and the parish (evaluation). A monitoring procedure makes a comparison between intent (what are the goals and objectives) and the performance (what actually happened). Discrepancies found to exist by this comparison constitute a need for developmental or remedial action.

A. *Supervision*

Supervision is a monitoring procedure for facilitating the progress and performance of individual persons.

1. *Summative Supervision:* Sensing-Thinking (ST) leaders prefer to use summative supervision. As supervisors they are the superordinates who

authoritatively inspect and judge the finished work of subordinates. Theirs is the final, summary judgment of the recognized authority.

2. *Active Supervision:* Sensing-Feeling (SF) leaders prefer to use this type of supervision. As supervisors they become actively involved in the work situation and concentrate on the factual data of what is happening here and now. They like to determine the best procedures and programs for growth for the person being supervised.

3. *Formative Supervision:* Intuitive-Feeling (NF) leaders act as facilitators of growth by imposing little formal structure or direction. They help the person to self-discovery, take the initiative to see that it occurs, and provide requested materials.

4. *Competency-based Supervision:* Intuitive-Thinking (NT) leaders plan a systematic growth process for "colleagues" in a joint determination about what competencies they wish to gain or improve within a specified period of time.

B. *Evaluation*

Evaluation is a monitoring procedure for making judgments about the progress and performance of the parish.

1. *Summative Evaluation:* Sensing-Thinking (ST) leaders assess the degree to which the parish's goals and objectives have been achieved in a summary, authoritative and judgmental manner.

2. *Active Evaluation:* Sensing-Feeling (SF) leaders use action-research methods to study the problems of the institution in order to guide, correct and evaluate decisions and actions of the institution. The approach is situational, i.e., each problem must be approached in each given parish. No effort is made to solve the problems for all situations. It is for this parish at this time.

3. *Formative Evaluation:* Intuitive-Feeling (NF) leaders use on-going monitoring systems that focus on discovering, describing and measuring important things that occur in the parish at various points. The function of formative evaluation is facilitative. It indicates the need for mid-stream changes and subsequent revisions.

4. *Competency-based Evaluation:* Intuitive-Thinking (NT) leaders list the standards and goals of the parish as criteria for self-study and evaluation. They judge the quality of implementation and achievement based on those pre-established criteria.

10

A Parish Plan of Action: 14 Leadership Skills

If parish leaders are to work synergistically with people, to share and solve problems with them, to clarify parish values and develop a shared vision, and to share power by collaborating with them in developing plans of action for the parish, innumerable acts of leadership are required. When parish leaders respond to the changing needs of people and to changing demographic and societal conditions, it is most likely that channels of communication remain open.

Many, many volumes have been written about communication. Untold numbers of communications courses have been taught and are being taught. Consequently, it is not our intention to teach the myriad skills and processes of interpersonal relations and verbal and non-verbal communication skills. It is our intention, however, to list and describe 14 interpersonal skills which effective leaders must possess. One of those leadership skills is the ability to understand and address organizational and communication patterns that are operative in the most effective and excellent companies in the United States. Leaders who can identify and understand these patterns can set out to establish them in their own parishes and dioceses, and in fact, in any institution.

I. Communicating with Different Personality-types

Usually a parish leadership team will be comprised of a variety and combination of personality-types: Sensing types (S's), Intuitive types (N's), Thinking types (T's), Feeling types (F's). Each type prefers to use a specific pattern of communicating.

When trying to communicate with an S and in order to get your message across, be certain that the content of the message is factual and practical; be certain that the process of communicating is direct, and that it does not rely on symbolism and abstract terms; be sure that all of the important details have been worked out thoroughly and presented explicitly. As sensing persons, they want the information to make practical sense. It makes more sense to them when the speaker or presenter can list and document specific successful incidents and applications. The less risk there is in implementing the message in their lives, the more likely it is that the S will "buy" it.

The exact opposite approach must be taken when trying to communicate with intuitives. In other words, do not rely on the above approach. Instead, the N's like challenges which require some risk taking. By exuding confidence in oneself and in the content of the message, the communicator can excite the N with what is being communicated. A global, abstract message is something that the N can easily understand. Stay away from a linear, line by line, item by item approach. The big picture which forecasts future benefits is what the N wants to hear.

S's and N's can be Thinking (T) or Feeling (F) persons. The T's want a logical presentation based on relevant principles. The communicator needs to be well organized in presenting both the facts for the S's and the possibilities for the N's. T's like well organized presentations to move logically from one point to the next point without any emotional issues distracting them from their logical thought processes. They need to hear the speaker stress the need for competency in dealing with important issues. The costs and benefits must be addressed also in order to convince T's that this is worth working for.

Feeling types (F's) are the opposite of T's. Consequently, the opposite approach must be used. F's want to hear an approach that is friendly, personable and full of feeling. Be certain to say that this is the "right" thing to do, not the logical thing to do. They want to know how this is going to help people, and that it is of value to people. When they are told that other people have been helped and that other people have indicated that they really like this, they will be sold. Anyone who stresses values, people and feelings will communicate well with F's.

Since there are four conbinations (ST, SF, NF, NT) it is not that difficult to communicate with most people. There usually is some common denominator that can be used in attracting different types of people to one message. The key to successful communication with each person in a group setting is to use a variety of approaches to help sell the major points of the issue at hand. The biggest problem, however, is that the less balanced (in type) they are, the more difficult it will be for them to accept differing points of view or a communication approach that does not fit their style. The challenge is to get differing types to "stretch," i.e., to hear and appreciate how other people understand what is being communicated. An effective communicator will address the facts, possibilities, logic and feelings to assure contact with each type.

II. Communicating by Brainstorming

Brainstorming is an efficient and quick way of generating ideas and feelings about a particular issue in small groups. If the issue for a leadership team is to explore what a parish's goals are, a facilitator would lead them through the following steps:

Step 1: Each team member is invited to express his/her goals for the parish without giving any kind of explanation. There is no time given in step one to analyze, describe, defend or evaluate the goals.

Step 2: All goals, no matter how ridiculous or crazy, are listened to and listed by a recorder.

Step 3: The team is seeking quantity, not quality, of ideas at this point.

Step 4: Each team member is invited by the facilitator to build on or modify the goals of others.

Step 5: Review and evaluate each parish goal.

Step 6: The facilitator would encourage team members to explore something of worth and soundness in every idea, even the seemingly craziest ones.

Step 7: All of the goals should be prioritized in order of importance to the group. (This involves a process of consensus.)

Step 8: The finished list of priorities is submitted to the appropriate persons or task force for review or approval.

Brainstorming can be used for each step of the action plan: for setting goals, objectives, strategies, time line, etc.

III. Communicating Through Consensus

When a team of people are expected to make a decision about what their parish goals and objectives are, the highest degree of ownership, involvement and active participation in working toward fulfilling those goals and objectives will occur when everyone is in agreement about those goals and objectives. The optimum way of arriving at a decision in a group is through consensus. *Consensus: each team member supports the final solution even though he or she may not agree totally, and everyone commits themselves to work toward what they have agreed upon.*

The following process has worked well for us in the past and we invite others to use it.

Step 1: Define and clarify the issue. Write on a chalk board or newsprint, visible and legible for everyone to see, exactly what the issue is. If it is a parish goal, objective, problem, or question, write it down.

Step 2: Invite each member of the group to ask questions which could clarify the written statement.

Step 3: Draw a horizontal line across the chalk board or newsprint:

_____

0   1   2   3   4   5   6   7   8   9

Step 4: Explain to the group that they are to decide how strongly they are in agreement or disagreement with the written statement.

Step 5: The facilitator invites each person individually to pick a number from 0-9 which represents his/her feelings and thoughts.

0 is complete disagreement.

1, 2 is strong disagreement.

3, 4 is some disagreement.

5, 6 is some agreement.

7, 8 is strong agreement.

9 is complete agreement.

Step 6: List the number of people who voted at each point (0-9) along the continuum.

Step 7: If everyone agrees, go on to the next issue. If everyone disagrees, throw out the issue.

Step 8: If team members express a variety of feelings and thoughts, ask the persons in the 3 to 6 range what they would modify or change in order to agree with the written statement.

Step 9: The facilitator now asks the people in the 0 to 2 range what they could live with, or what the next most acceptable alternative is for them. It is important to focus on what everyone can agree on.

Step 10: The facilitator continues to work for a statement of the issue which *everyone* can live with and actively support. The facilitator watches for signs of agreement, rewrites the original statement as often as necessary, and continues to change the listed number of people at each point of the continuum on the chalk board. The facilitator constantly encourages members to do what is the best and what is right for the parish and try to put aside individual agendas.

Step 11: If consensus is impossible, ask the dissenters to write a minority report stating their positions.

IV. Communicating through Paraphrasing

Most people assume that they understand what the other person said without indicating to the speaker what has been said or understood. Paraphrasing is a method of "proving" to other people how you have understood their message. Repeating in your own words what you think they said gives them an opportunity to clarify or agree with your interpretation of their message.

V. Communicating by Checking Impressions

When you use sentences that begin with the words *"You feel"* (happy, sad, frustrated, angry, overjoyed, confused, etc.) or *"because"* (you were not invited, your idea was not logical, you don't have all the facts, your values are different from mine, etc.) you can help listeners check the emotional state of another person and the reason for that emotional state. By stating one's impressions in this way, a person can determine whether he/she is "reading" the right message from actual spoken words, facial expressions, non-verbal gestures or verbal tones of voice. The purpose of checking your own impressions of someone's verbal or non-verbal message is to assure other persons that you really are interested in knowing and appreciating their thoughts and feelings.

VI. Communicating by Describing the Behavior of Others

Most people find it difficult to describe accurately another person's behavior so that the other person will understand what specific actions are affecting their relationship. To do this well, leaders must observe what happened without making inferences, evaluations or judgments, and describe the actions with clarity and specificity. This method helps people in talking about their relationship and how behavior affects it.

VII. Communicating by Describing One's Own Feelings

The purpose of describing your own feelings to another person is to initiate a dialogue whereby the other person or persons know how you feel in order to improve a relationship. Getting in touch with and describing your own feelings should be done with clarity and specificity.

VIII. Communicating by Listening

For many people it is probably more difficult to listen than it is to talk. Listening requires concentration to understand how people really feel, what people are really saying and what needs they have that they are trying to convey to us.

IX. Communicating by Resolving Conflicts through Confrontation

In a confrontation, one person directly expresses his/her view and feelings about the conflict. She always invites the other person to express her views and feelings about the conflict. The purpose is to resolve the problem. However, *do not confront* if the following conditions exist:

- the relationship is not healthy or strong enough.
- the anxiety level is too high at that time.
- the willingness to change is clearly not present.
- the other person is not ready or able to respond constructively.

When the conditions are right, the following steps can be taken in resolving conflicts:

Step 1: Time is needed to resolve conflicts. Be certain that both persons have the time to work through the process.

Step 2: Both persons explore and define how they see the conflict.

Step 3: Both persons must discuss their feelings, thoughts and perceptions about the underlying issues of the problem. They must do this honestly and without threats and emotional outbursts. They must try to focus their emotions on the issue at hand.

Step 4: Each person must try to understand the other's thoughts, feelings and perceptions.

Step 5: Try to negotiate ways to resolve the conflict and to form a more effective relationship. Neither person, however, should demand changes in behavior from the other person. Changes may be requested and negotiated, not demanded.

These five steps constitute an outline of the confrontational process. Parish leaders must learn interpersonal skills and practice them in order to enhance the quality of the parish and the satisfaction level of parishioners.

X. Communicating Through A Synergistic Problem Solving Process

A problem is the discrepancy between what is and how we would like it to be. A problem can be viewed in a positive or negative sense, just as a math problem can be positive $(2 + 2 = 4)$ or negative $(4 - 2 = 2)$. A positive problem can be seen as a challenge to be met. A negative problem is a problem to be solved. Our mental outlook on problems can drain or invigorate us. If discrepancies are healthy tensions that create challenge for continued growth and progress, life can be more interesting, transforming and meaningful. If discrepancies are problems to be avoided and reluctantly dealt with, life can be oppressive, defensive and depressing.

A healthy approach is to share those problems which mutually affect us. In doing so we are saying to one another: "You and your needs mean something to me. I am willing to listen to you. I feel important too because you are willing to listen to me express my needs and concerns about this issue which affects my life and yours. Let's look at this problem together from our varied perspectives." Parish leaders can take seven steps in a synergistic problem solving process.

Step 1: The leader selects the right people to be members of the problem solving leadership team. These are the people who are directly affected by the final solution. If there are an inordinate number of people who fit this category, representatives of each constituency should be invited to participate. The leader should be aware of the different strengths and weaknesses of each personality-type represented in the group. This helps the leader create a synergistic approach in solving problems. The leader empowers each person to contribute his/her strengths in solving the problem.

Step 2: The leadership team identifies and agrees on the right problem. Each person in the group is empowered to address the problem that has been identified by the leader or by a member of the group. Each person in the group is invited by the facilitator to explore whether or not the proposed problem is truly a problem.

Each person is invited to supply data and reasons to support the contention that this is or is not a problem. Each team member may offer an opinion from his/her own perspective: ST

                    NT   ST

                         NF

ST: supplies data, facts and information; may indicate that a policy or rule was not followed and that the expectations of the diocese or parish have not been met. *SF*: supplies dimension of feeling and values as well as factual data; looks at both individual's needs and Church expectations. *NF*: speaks to social aspects of problem; what are the effects of the problem and of the solution on individuals and on the community. *NT*: may point to what is wrong with the system; will help bring definition and logic to the problem.

Step 3: Each member of the problem solving task team is invited to brainstorm possible solutions. Each person can contribute to the formation of the final solution by offering a variety of alternative suggestions.

ST: usually offers solutions that have worked in the past; suggests the use of standard procedures; solutions are based on company regulations or criteria. *SF*: offers solutions which benefit the organization while being sensitive to the feelings of individuals. *NF*: offers creative solutions based on personal beliefs and commonly accepted community values. *NT*: offers creative solutions based on intellectual theories; envisions organizational change to prevent problems.

Step 4: The team prioritizes the list of solutions according to how well they fulfill the needs of all parties who are affected by the problem and the solution.

Step 5: Each group member lists the forces that support and constrain their efforts in implementing the proposed solutions.

Examples of positive forces could be the following: sufficient financial support, parish has excellent ministries to fulfill needs of parishioners, a geographic area which is attracting new industries and new people. Examples of negative forces could be the following: parish with few parishioners; parish in geographic area with declining numbers of residents; parish is not able to provide ministries to help people.

Step 6: Action procedures are agreed to by all the members. Goals, objectives, strategies, etc. are agreed to and implemented.

Step 7: Supervision of persons who are implementing the action plan *and evaluation of progress* is scheduled in the calendar of activities. Information that is gathered from supervision and evaluation is needed to assure quality of performance and productive results.

XI. Communicating Through Decision Making

A. A Synergistic Process for Decision Making

It is a well founded theory that the best decisions are made as close to the point of delivery as possible. Research indicates that decision making is usually decentralized in effective organizations. A decision is more acceptable when people who are directly affected by the decision have had input, influence on and ownership of the decision. Increased participation increases the chances for acceptance and consensus in the institution. It gives followers and workers a significant amount of information about the Vision and Spirit of the organization. The satisfaction level of individuals and the level of their cooperation increases. Burnout and boreout can be prevented.

Knowing all of these wonderful things that result from participative and synergistic decision making, it is incredible that more leaders of institutions have not made the necessary changes to adopt this important and effective process.

The design of any institution's structure should include levels of decision making that are consistent with each person's realm of responsibility. When people know what their responsibilities are, and when they know what power and authority they possess for decision making, frustration and embarrassment can be avoided.

Every institution needs a formal decision making structure which permits individuals to make routine and ordinary daily decisions. In ordinary situations which usually require repetitive routine answers collaboration is unnecessary because this type of decision making demands no new solutions.

However, synergistic decision making processes can be used in parishes in the following situations:

• when the parish needs input from several different representatives of various constituencies. They should be invited to share their specific competencies, knowledge and experience in working toward solutions for particular problems or challenges;

• when the parish wants to build personal ownership for specific issues;

• when multiple options and perspectives are needed;

• when the decisions affect the future (Vision) of the parish;

• when a process is needed for making decisions which should involve people throughout the parish.

Synergistic decision making teams will be successful when they take the following specific steps to help them achieve their task.

Step 1: establish clear parameters about who makes specific decisions in certain areas and situations;

Step 2: assign relevant and manageable tasks;

Step 3: set a definite time line;

Step 4: determine processes and relationships for reporting progress;

Step 5: include all the people (or their representatives) who will be directly affected by the decision;

Step 6: create procedures to assure public awareness, recognition and reward for the team's efforts;

Step 7: inform team members and the public about how the group was formed and the process for dissolving the team;

Step 8: establish an understanding about how decisions will be made and used;

Step 9: make a distinction, if necessary, between authority to make final decisions and genuine influence in decision making;

Step 10: be clearly aware of the issue of "decisional deprivation." This is the difference between the amount of involvement persons think they *should have* in decision making and the amount they *actually have.*

B. Making Decisions by Gathering Sufficient Information

"Vigilant information processing" is a process that Sensing (S) decision makers would use when they or their parish is involved in making an important decision. In the opinion of James and Mann, all decision makers usually find themselves in the following situations. And, they routinely do not process information adequately in these situations. This approach suggests that decisions should be made only after all of the information is gathered and vigilantly processed.

Situation #1: The risks to continue what the parish has been doing seem rather low. Consequently, the parish will probably continue to do the same thing and will not see the need to gather information about other possible alternatives.

Situation #2: The risks in continuing what the parish has been doing seem rather high, and the risks of an obvious alternative seem low. Consequently, the parish will probably select the obvious alternative without gathering information about other possible alternatives.

Situation #3: All of the current obvious alternatives look risky. The decision makers in the parish believe they have little opportunity in coming up with a better alternative. So, they will indicate that no problem exists, or they will exaggerate the advantages of the alternative solution they picked, or they'll try to get someone else to make the decision.

Situation #4: The decision makers in the parish feel that, potentially, they can find an adequate alternative decision. However, they also feel that it will disappear by the time it will take to explore other alternatives. Then, they'll probably panic.

Situation #5: The parish decision makers think that all of their obvious alternative decisions are risky. However, they will take the time that is needed to explore a better choice. In this case, they can involve themselves in "vigilant information processing."

C. Intuitive Decision Making

This is the completely opposite approach for making decisions from the approach just described, "vigilant information processing." In a fascinating little book with a long title, *Intuitive Management, Integrating Left and Right Brain Management Skills, How to Make the Right Decision at the Right Time,* Weston H. Agor suggests that we rely on our intuition for making decisions. According to Agor, we usually arrive at decisions which are just as good or better in a shorter period of time when we use our intuition, and without collecting and processing all kinds of information and data.

> Frequently in life, we have an intuitive understanding of a person or a situation. But, normally we are afraid to act on the basis of this instant awareness of our feelings. Instead, we fall back to the tape we have often been socialized to program, 'You had better wait, gather more facts, get to know the person or situation better.' So, we delay our actions and our decisions.... Intuition, fully developed, then, is a highly efficient way of knowing. It is fast and accurate. Our system will process a wide array of information on many levels, and give us an instantaneous cue how to act. We have the answer even though we do not understand all the steps, or know fully all the information our system processed to give us this cue.[1]

XII. Institutional Communication Patterns

The parish must exist for people. The diocese must exist for people. In fact, all institutions must exist for people. Within the *excellent* institutions that actually do exist for people, there are certain undeniable characteristics that set them apart from the mediocre institutions. Within the excellent institutions people share knowledge with one another and try to keep everyone informed. In other words, they communicate well. Persons in excellent institutions also try to form supportive communities by genuinely responding to one another's needs. Excellent institutions, those of real quality, establish a caring climate and the conditions which help people transform their lives and their work into something better. And, when quality institutions and their people see the need to re-form whatever needs to be reformed, their leaders lead their followers to make efforts to achieve excellence, holiness or perfection.

The larger and more complex the institution (like a diocese), the more important it becomes for leaders not only to establish clear, formal channels for moving information, but also to create informal opportunities which invite and encourage people to communicate.

Leaders of every institution can learn a lot about their institution when they take the time to observe the current operative structure of communication patterns. They must look at the formal and informal structures at different levels and subsystems of the organization. Formal channels of communication are those official ways that information is shared, discussed or moved: diocesan meetings, deanery meetings, departmental meetings, newsletters, official letters, announcements, newspaper articles, etc. Informal channels of communication are those unofficial ways that information is shared, discussed or moved: golf outings, dinners, informal discussions, coffee breaks, management by walking around (MBWA), etc.

Throughout this book we have emphasized the complementary differences of people. We have tried to demonstrate in this chapter that individual persons actually do use different patterns of communication depending on their personality-types. It is our belief that institutions also use specific communication patterns which arise out of their corporate personality-type (a combination of their Vision, Spirit, and type of Power that is emphasized).

Church leaders and followers can study the current communication patterns in operation in their diocese or parish. They can also study the following list of organizational and communication patterns that are actually found in the best and the most excellent companies in the United States.

After each statement, the reader may quickly check "true" (this is true of my parish or diocese, or the organization of your choice) or "false" (this is not true of my parish or diocese, or organization of your choice). Make a judgment about the place where you work or where you pray. Make a judgment about whether this particular condition exists in whatever organization or institution you would like to evaluate for excellence. The following 40 statements should give you clues about *what you might be able to do to make it excellent*.

1. Peters and Waterman report in their book, *The Pursuit of Excellence,* that the nature and uses of communication in companies they have judged to be excellent are significantly different from the nonexcellent companies. The excellent companies emphasize and depend on a huge network of informal, open communications. Patterns of informality and openness encourage the right people to get into contact with the other right people on a regular basis.

true __ false __

2. The intensity of informal communications is unmistakable in the excellent companies.

true __ false __

3. Open door policies not only exist but are practiced.

true __ false __

4. In *non-excellent* companies, people are almost never in face-to-face communication, except at formal meetings.

true __ false __

5. The quality of performance almost always improves when one individual person or a subgroup within a group has contact with everyone else in the group.

true __ false __

6. The institution has developed the dual ability to coordinate people, plus the ability to create new structures, incentives and a new philosophy of leadership.

true __ false __

7. The characteristics of excellent institutions tend to bring out the best in people. And, it should be noted that all of their characteristics deal with human relationships.

true __ false __

8. Productivity comes from coordination of people (synergy) rather than from increased individual effort.

true __ false __

9. Institutions cannot reform their people. The institution must change, if necessary, their internal social structure in such a way that it meets the individual needs of people and fulfills the expectations of the institution.

true __ false __

10. Excellent institutions have "link-pin" structures. A person or sub-group functions in this way when they participate in two or more separate communication networks. In this way they are able to share information up, down, and across groups that usually do not communicate with each other.

true __ false __

11. Leaders in excellent institutions provide their followers and workers with the means for success. They do this by effective coordination of persons, a guarantee of needed resources to accomplish the task, inviting them to share in decision making about matters that directly affect their work, ministry and life. They encourage dialogue on issues that are central to the institution's purpose.

true __ false __

12. People in excellent institutions talk to one another a lot without requiring loads of paper work and formality.

true __ false __

13. Leaders generate opportunities for their people to celebrate.

true __ false __

14. Leaders generate opportunities for their people to exchange good news.

true __ false __

15. Honor people at the "top" and "bottom" of the institution who have made valuable contributions with different kinds of positive reinforcement and rewards.

true __ false __

16. Meaningful informal communication helps people stay in touch and on top of things, and leads to more action.

true __ false __

17. Excellent institutions have a flexible and fluid organization which depends on task teams rather than on committees with fragmented responsibilities.

true __ false __

18. Excellent institutions do not focus on upper levels, such as departments and business units, which are listed on formal organization charts. They use small groups (8-10 persons) to form their basic organizational building blocks. For instance, 3M has several hundred 4-10 person teams. A successful Australian company, ICI, has a multitude of interlocking teams.

true __ false __

19. The necessity of open and intense communications in the institution is emphasized at IBM:

> Contact among members was intense; all principal players met in conference for a half day each week to review progress and decide on changes. Minutes were published within less than twelve hours. Everyone on the project had access to all the information he needed: every programmer, for instance, saw all the material coming from every group on the project. Nobody who attended the weekly meetings came in an advisory (i.e., staff) role. Everyone had the authority to make binding commitments.[2]

true __ false __

20. Excellent institutions possess a willingness to experiment.

true __ false __

21. They see themselves as an extended family

true __ false __

22. People in excellent institutions use a typically private language. In fact, when they begin to discuss their institutional philosophy and values, there is a pretty good chance they will start to live it. However, at first, the words of the philosophy may not have much meaning for them.

true __ false __

23. Excellent institutions use slogans, phrases and a set of symbols that tend to upgrade the image of their individual workers and produce a higher level of productivity.

true __ false __

24. Excellent institutions do not rigidly follow a chain of command in day-to-day communication. However, they do rely on it for major decisions.

true __ false __

25. Informality and wandering around are critical leadership strategies.

true __ false __

26. On-going training activities are made available.

true __ false __

27. A steady and meaningful supply of information down through the ranks prevents low morale.

true __ false __

28. Excellent institutions use an abundance of non-monetary incentives which are powerful positive reinforcement strategies.

true __ false __

29. What is evaluated and measured is accomplished and completed.

true __ false __

30. Interchanging people and jobs is a fundamental principle.

true __ false __

31. Excellent institutions seek and achieve "smallness." People can more easily understand something small, manage it more easily and be committed to it.

true __ false __

32. Large, complex institutions that have achieved excellence act like a group of smaller institutions which have been given a lot of independence and the needed resources to be successful.

true __ false __

33. In this type of institution (31 & 32), individual persons feel and are valuable. They are able to stand out in this structure. They feel like they can make a difference. There are more opportunities for face to face communication and informality.

true __ false __

34. The most significant aspect of the "small" institution is the team. In most of the companies that were *not* on the list of Peters and Waterman, the strategic business unit was

> considered the basic building block of the organization. Among our winners the team is the crucial factor, regardless of the issue—service, innovation, or productivity.[3]

true __ false __

35. Every opportunity is found to celebrate team achievements.

true __ false __

36. Individual persons are most productive and can be themselves only in small, comprehensible groups.

true __ false __

37. We respect the individual person.

true __ false __

38. We make persons feel like winners.

true __ false __

39. We treat persons like adults.

true __ false __

40. We let persons stand out.

true __ false __

As the reader can readily see, effective communication is directly tied into the organizational structure of the institution. And, for us, communication is much more than "giving and receiving information." Communication means that people are in communion with one another through their behavior, their lived values, their institutional vision, their shared use of power and the way the institution is structured. Keeping people informed, forming relationships and a sense of community, transforming people through caring service and re-forming organizations to respect and respond to people's priority needs is what we mean by communication.

This is an awesome and awful responsibility for those leaders who perch themselves on top of the hierarchical structure to be the lone chief. For those leadership teams who can communicate well and act interdependently, the fruit of their synergistic labors will be sweet and fulfilling.

11

Conclusion

Once we are convinced of the need to respond to our own specific parish situation, the obvious question is "What are we going to do about it?" The parishes that respond positively and enthusiastically to the challenges of the present and future will be parishes where parishioners, priests and religious men and women are willing to work together for a common purpose and vision.

Because the world is not static, but dynamic, parish leaders are challenged to prepare their individual parishioners and communal parishes for the future. Both, the organizational aspect and the revitalization aspect must be forward looking. Parish leaders will need encouragement and help in leading and facilitating needed change. Their commitment to the future must be rooted in the theological virtue of hope and in the promise of Christ who said, "I will be with you all days, even to the end of time." Parish leaders who are filled with hope will look forward to the future with confidence. They will be able to instill in their parishioners this same confidence and hope. By their attitudes, style and degree of commitment, they will testify that no task is too big or too difficult to undertake if they believe that the grace of God which builds on human nature will strengthen and sustain them.

We, laity, clergy and religious, are being asked to bring Christ to people of our time through a divinely instituted Church which also happens to be a human institution. We are being sent on a mission to make His Kingdom a relevant reality in our time and culture.

Priests, parishioners and religious men and women, as a team, can develop and implement a parish plan of action to re-form any aspect of the parish that is in need of reorganizing and revitalizing. They may select and use a variety of phases, processes and skills depending upon the challenge that faces them. A parish plan of action will provide efficient, effective, affective and creative processes for bringing new life to parishes and parishioners. Each parish plan of action should be reviewed and evaluated periodically in order to gather information about maintaining, modifying, changing or discontinuing the plan. This will assure the relevancy and effectiveness of the plan as demographics and needs change. It will help the changing American parish meet the changing needs of parishioners and society. It will become a parish full of life and vitality. It will become an animated parish.

Appendix A

"Personality-Type" Check List

This check-list is divided into four sections. The statements in the first section address your preference for Introversion (I) or Extra-version (E). The statements in the second section address your preference for Intuition (N) or Sensing (S); the third section: Thinking (T) or Feeling (F); the fourth section: Judging (J) or Perceiving (P).

Each set of statements refers to opposite preferences: introversion versus extraversion; intuition versus sensing, etc. You are being forced to decide between the two in each set of statements. Check one statement in each set. Answer all the statements even though some decisions might be difficult.

The statements are based on the personality-type theories of Carl Jung, Myers-Briggs and Kiersey-Bates. There are no incorrect answers, and each personality-type is a good, healthy type. To begin to help you understand whether you prefer I or E, S or N, T or F, J or P check the statement in each set which describes you and your behavior best. You will gain some insights about yourself through this checklist. If you would like to gain a deeper understanding about yourself, you are encouraged to complete the "Myers-Briggs Type Indicator" (MBTI) which is available from the "Center for Application of Psychological Types" in Gainesville, Florida. The use of the MBTI will provide a more valid and accurate description of one's personality-type.

I.   *Introversion Preferences*   *Extraversion Preferences*

I PREFER: OR   I PREFER:

1. __ a. to be alone or with a friend or two.   __ b. to be with a lot of and a variety of friends.

2. __ a. to act carefully when trying something new.   __ b. to act spontaneously and quickly.

3. __ a. to know what is expected of me.   __ b. to set my own standards.

4. __ a. to have a few social relationships.   __ b. to have multiple social relationships.

5. __ a. to do a few things and do them well.   __ b. to do a variety of things and maybe not do them all very well.

6. __ a. quiet time.   __ b. a lot of activity.

7. __ a. concentration.   __ b. interaction.

8. __ a. spending time with one person or a few people at gatherings.   __ b. "mixing" with people and "table hopping."

9. __ a. turning inward to myself and ideas.   __ b. outward to people and things.

10.   a. I am an Introvert: b. I am an Extravert:
     __ almost always.   __ almost always.
     __ usually.   __ usually.
     __ occasionally.   __ occasionally.
     __ rarely.   __ rarely.
     __ almost never.   __ almost never.

II.   *Intuition Preferences*   *Sensing Preferences*

I PREFER: OR   I PREFER:

1. __ a. to go with my hunches and   __ b. to depend on informa-
        intuition.   and correct data.

2. __ a. ideas and possibilities.   __ b. facts and realities.

3. __ a. to feel that nothing is   __ b. to be realistic about
        impossible if only given   things.
        enough time.

4. __ a. to deal with what is   __ b. to deal with what has
        possible.   actually happened.

5. __ a. a vision for the future.   __ b. the wisdom of the past.

6. __ a. to use inspiration when   __ b. to use perspiration when
        doing a job.   doing a job.

7. __ a. new ways of doing things   __ b. the standard ways of
        and dislike doing the same   doing things and don't mind
        thing over.   repetition.

8. __ a. creative, future.   __ b. past, practical, facts.

9. __ a. to change things.   __ b. to accept things as they are.

10. __a. I am impatient with details, __ b. I am patient with   fine
        print and directions.   detals, fine print and directions.

11   a. I am an Intuitive person: b. I am a Sensing person:
        __ almost always   __ almost always.
        __ usually.   __ usually.
        __ occasionally.   __ occasionally.
        __ rarely.   __ rarely.
        __ almost never.   __ almost never.

III.   *Thinking Preferences*   *Feeling Preferences*

       I PREFER: OR   I PREFER:

1. __ a.to rely on my thinking abilities when making decisions.

__ b. to rely on my feelings when making decisions.

2. __ a. justice.

__ b. mercy.

3. __ a. to take a firm stand on things.

__ b. to give in to others for the sake of peace.

4. __ a. law and policies.

__ b. sympathy and forgiveness.

5. __ a. order.

__ b. harmony.

6. __ a. to believe in firmness.

__ b. to believe there are extenuating circumstances.

7. __ a. logic, thinking and being objective.

__ b. feelings, values and being personal.

8. __ a. Arguments do not upset me.

__ b. Arguments do upset me.

9. __ a. I may neglect the feelings of other people.

__ b. I try to be aware of the feelings of others.

10. __a. Sometimes I tend to be "hardheaded."

__ b. Sometimes I tend to be "softhearted."

11 a. I think I am a thinking person:
__ almost always.
__ usually.
__ occasionally.
__ rarely.
__ almost never.

b. I feel I am a feeling person:
__ almost always.
__ usually.
__ occasionally.
__ rarely.
__ almost never.

IV. *Judging Preferences*   *Perceiving Preferences*

I PREFER: OR   I PREFER:

1. __ a. to settle things.   __ b. to keep my options open.

2. __ a. to make decisions quickly.   __ b. to make decisions by taking my time.

3. __ a. the structured and scheduled.   __ b. the unstructured and unscheduled.

4. __ a. to start and finish things.   __ b. to start several projects even though I have trouble finishing them.

5. __ a. to make things come out the way they ought to be.   __ b. to have things evolve.

6. __ a. closure to meetings and things.   __ b. to be open-minded.

7. __ a. the words: decided, settled, fixed   __ b. the words: pending, flexible, gathering more information.

8. __ a. to plan ahead.   __ b. to adapt as I go.

9. __ a. to be decisive.   __ b. to "go with the flow."

10. __a. I usually have my mind made up.   __ b. I usually look for added information.

11.   a. I judge myself to be a judging person: b. I perceive myself to be a perceiving person:
        __ almost always.   __ almost always.
        __ usually.   __ usually.
        __ occasionally.   __ occasionally.
        __ rarely.   __ rarely.
        __ almost never.   __ almost never.

PERSONALITY-TYPE ANSWER SHEET

	I or E	N or S	T or F	J or P
Question:				
1.	_a _b	_a _b	_a _ b	_a _b
2.	_a _b	_a _b	_a _b	_a _b
3.	_a _b	_a _b	_a _ b	_a _b
4.	_a _b	_a _b	_a _ b	_a _b
5.	_a _b	_a _b	_a _ b	_a _b
6.	_a _b	_a _b	_a _ b	_a _b
7.	_a _b	_a _b	_a _ b	_a _b
8.	_a _b	_a _b	_a _ b	_a _b
9.	_a _b	_a _b	_a _ b	_a _b
10.	_a _b	_a _b	_a _ b	_a _b
11.	_a _b	_a _b	_a _ b	_a _b

Count each check-mark for one point and add the points in each of the eight columns and enter eight totals. This will give you an insight into your preferences.

_|_   _|_   _|_   _|_

Appendix B

"Church-Type" Checklist

We have different concepts about what the church/parish is and what it should be in today's world. You are being asked in this checklist to think about the "type" of parish/church you prefer. Answer each question completely. There are no wrong answers. You are being forced to make choices and some of the choices will not be easy ones. However, please make them.

For each question from 1 to 13, rate each of the four answers with a 1, 2, 3 and 4 in order of preference and priority. Enter all four answers in columns a, b, c and d on the "Church-Type Answer Sheet" (page 188).

1. I prefer this answer over the other three answers.

2. I prefer this answer next.

3. I prefer this answer third.

4. I prefer this answer last.

1. The Parish's/Church's mission is to:

    a.   give eternal life to its members.

    b.   be of help to all persons everywhere; to maintain the Church's values; to offer guidance, support and wisdom.

    c.   lead men and women into communion with God here on earth and in heaven.

    d.   help people reform their lives and convert them to the gospels.

2. The Parish/Church becomes a living sign in the world when it:

    a.   maintains official structures and gives clear directives.

    b.   cares for people through acts of charitable service.

    c.   acts as a community of loving people.

    d.   stands against the world as a sign of contradiction.

3. The Parish/Church must:

    a.   be a structured institution and remain the kind of institution Christ started.

    b.   help human society through service based on gospel values.

    c.   be lovingly united to one another and to God in a community of prayer and worship.

    d.   purify itself of its faults and be holy.

4. As a parishioner I believe that the Parish/Church should stress:

    a.   the Church's official teaching.

    b.   charitable deeds for others.

    c.   the need for a united community.

    d.   reform and renewal.

5. The purpose of the Sacrifice of the Mass is to:

    a.   carry out Christ's mandate to his apostles at the Last Supper.

    b.   move people to serve the needs of others after being strengthened by the Eucharist.

    c.   form a community of faithful people with the Eucharist as their focal point.

    d.   remind people that they and the Church must remain relevant to the message of the Eucharist.

6. A priest's primary function is to:

    a.   act as the official representative of Christ's Church.

    b.   offer the service of the Church to the needy.

    c.   help unite people to God and to one another.

    d.   help reform secular society through continual reminders about Christian values.

7. The bond(s) which unite us in the Church is (are):

    a.   a humble compliance with Church dogma.

    b.   a sense of mutual responsibility that results in Christian service to the world.

    c.   the gifts of the Holy Spirit which help form a faithful people.

    d.   the Church's ability to remain true to its calling of holiness.

8. People who benefit from belonging to the Church are:

    a.   Catholics in good standing in the Church.

    b.   persons the world over who receive from the Church comfort, encouragement, care amd help in their times of need.

    c.   those who are in contact with the believing and loving   Church.

    d.   people who want to become holy through personal renewal.

9. Salvation is possible for me if:

    a.   I obey and follow the teachings of the Church.

    b.   I help other people with selfless and charitable service.

    c.   I live my life based on personal relationships founded on mutual understanding and love.

    d.   I am holy.

10. The statement which best attests to my kind of Church is:

    a.   "You are Peter and on this Rock I will build my Church."

    b.   "I have come to serve and not to be served."

    c.   "You know they are Christians by their love."

    d.   "I have come not to bring peace but division into the world."

11. I believe that the Church should be primarily:

    a.   Authority: the official Church who teaches, rules and sanctifies.

    b.   Servant: as Jesus came to serve and not to be served, so   must the Church serve others.

    c.   Community: a Spirit-filled community whose people live a fellowship of life, charity and truth.

    d.   Prophet: to scrutinize the signs of the times and interpret them in the light of the gospels.

12. I prefer the type of Church which is:

    a.   Apostolic: a Church that remains in visible apostolic continuity with its own origins.

    b.   Catholic: a Church that reaches out to people everywhere and serves them by fulfilling their needs.

    c.   One: a Church whose members live together in one community of faith, trust and mutual concern.

    d.   Holy: a Church which gives grace to people to live holy lives.

13. I prefer the type of Church which:

    a.   uses its authority in fulfilling its official duties and obligations for the good of the Church and its faithful members.

    b.   serves the highest priority needs of people by offering the Church's resources to them.

    c.   builds a community where people live shared values in a common life.

    d.   honestly critiques contemporary society and reminds people to be true to their calling as Christians.

"CHURCH-TYPE" ANSWER SHEET

QUESTION	ANSWERS
	a l b l c l d
1.	_l_l_l_
2.	_l_l_l_
3.	_l_l_l_
4.	_l_l_l_
5.	_l_l_l_
6.	_l_l_l_
7.	_l_l_l_
8.	_l_l_l_
9.	_l_l_l_
10.	_l_l_l_
11.	_l_l_l_
12.	_l_l_l_
13.	_l_l_l_

Add the numbers down in each column so that there is a total for a, b, c and d.   _l_l_l_

The lowest total indicates what type of Church you prefer most.

The highest total indicates what type of Church you prefer least.

Column "a": "Apostolic" Church.

Column "b": "Catholic" Church.

Column "c": "One" Church.

Column "d": "Holy" Church.

Appendix C

"Church Leadership-Type" Answer Sheet

Completing this checklist may help you understand your own preferences for Church leadership: the way you lead or how you expect your leaders to lead. Members of the same leadership team, or leaders/followers in the same organization may receive insights about why they are able or not able to work well together. Different leadership preferences can lead to problems. However, the differences can be valuable, helpful and complementary when people rely on each other's strengths in a synergistic way. Consequently, the results from this checklist may help leaders and leadership teams begin to understand their leadership styles, to discuss them, and to use their new-found knowledge to lead more effectively.

Please answer each question completely. For each question from 1-13, rate each of the four answers with a 1, 2, 3, and 4 in order of your preference and priority. Enter all four answers in columns a, b, c and d on the "Church Leadership-Type Answer Sheet" (page 193).

1. I prefer this answer over the other three answers.

2. I prefer this answer next.

3. I prefer this answer third.

4. I prefer this answer last.

1. I appreciate Parish/Church leaders for:

a. the carefulness, thoroughness, and commitment to their   work.
b. the help they give people in need.
c. their personal expressions of appreciation and concern.
d. their intelligence, ideas and competence in their work.

2. I appreciate Parish/Church leaders who are:

a. loyal and industrious.
b. responsive and serving.
c. unique persons making unique contributions.
d. capable and talented.

3. I become irritated when Church leaders:

a. do not employ standard operating procedures.
b. tell people how to do things.
c. treat people impersonally.
d. ask people to do something illogical.

4. I appreciate Church leaders who:

a. conserve the past, and establish rules, regulations and procedures.
b. are involved with people in their practical problems.
c. are personally committed to the people they lead.
d. have vision, can conceptualize and give direction for the future.

5. When advocating change, Church leaders should be:

a. focusing on ways of doing things according to clearly defined lines of authority, facts and tradition.
b. able to mobilize for action when problems occur.
c. persuasive, verbal and outspoken, making appeals through emotion laden positions.
d. intelligent and competent with the ability to design models for change.

6. I appreciate Church leaders who:

a.   lend stability and confidence.

b.   lend practical help from the resources of the institution.

c.   work at interpersonal relationships with people.

d.   provide vision and theoretical models.

7. Bishops and pastors must:

a.   focus on Church organization and have the ability to establish policies, rules, regulations and hierarchy.

b.   fulfill the needs of the Church and the individuals in it.

c.   focus on individuals within the organization and their personal growth.

d.   get people to follow them because of their dreams and vision.

8. Church leaders should focus their ministry on:

a.   preserving the faith, tradition and culture of the Church.

b.   solving problems that exist in society.

c.   interacting with people in their daily lives.

d.   building a better world for the future.

9. Decisions in the Parish Church which directly affect the parishioners should be made by:

a.   the pastor alone.

b.   the pastor alone after consultation with the parish council.

c.   consensus between pastor and parish council.

d.   the pastor in negotiation with the involved persons.

10. Church leaders should:

a.   have a sense of tradition and authority, and identify with the history of the Church.

b.   have a sense of action, and move the Church to do charitable things for others.

c.   be interested in the future and try to help determine where God is leading individuals, the Church and the world.

d.   emphasize the importance of intellect and personal competence over other human faculties and skills.

11. Church leaders should:

a. carry out their obligation to implement faith into action.
b. emphasize Christian action to serve others, while appealing to a sense of duty.
c. build God's kingdom here on earth through community.
d. know Christian theology and relay its relevancy to people.

12. In order of priority, Church leaders should emphasize:

a. Christian duty.
b. charitable action.
c. a harmonious community.
d. vision for an enduring Church.

13. In order to help people grow, Church leaders should encourage their followers to:

a. examine their spiritual track records and decide what changes are needed in their spiritual lives.
b. recognize and accept the challenges that confront them every day.
c. open themselves to Christ and decide what new directions their spiritual journeys might take.
d. understand the Truth and experience Divine Wisdom.

"CHURCH LEADERSHIP-TYPE" ANSWER SHEET

QUESTION	ANSWERS
	a l b l c l d
1.	_l_l_ l_
2.	_l_l_ l_
3.	_l_l_ l_
4.	_l_l_ l_
5.	_l_l_ l_
6.	_l_l_ l_
7.	_l_l_ l_
8.	_l_l_ l_
9.	_l_l_ l_
10.	_l_l_ l_
11.	_l_l_ l_
12.	_l_l_ l_
13.	_l_l_ l_

Add the numbers down in each column so that there is a total for a, b, c and d: _l_l_ l_

The lowest total indicates what type of leadership-type you prefer most.

The highest total indicates what type you prefer least:

Column "a": evolving from "ST" & "Authority" type of leadership.

Column "b": evolving from "SF" & "Servant" type of leadership.

Column "c": evolving from "NF" & "Community" type of leadership.

Column "d": evolving from "NT" & "Prophet" type of leadership.

Appendix D

How Parish Leaders Can Facilitate Change

This approach for helping parishioners through change views change as a process rather than an event. It examines the various motivations, perceptions, attitudes, and feelings experienced by individuals in relation to change.

Like other institutions in our complex society, the Church must cope with constantly accelerating changes and increasingly pressing needs. There have been a number of responses from a few dioceses. Some have not yet begun to meet the challenge. Clearly, there is a need for a mechanism to help Church personnel and parishioners respond to the difficult task to change and to adapt effectively.

We have adapted the *Concerns-Based Adoption Model (CBAM)*[1] from an educational setting to a parish setting. A major dimension of this model is the psychological orientation of the individual toward change. The change agents (pastor and parish leaders) can use certain interventions to help people through the change process.

The term "concerns" is used to represent a composite description of the various motivations, perceptions, attitudes, feelings, and mental gyrations experienced by a person in relation to a change.

Facilitating change means that at least one or two persons have some informal or formal responsibility to assist the diocese and the parish toward needed change.

Change is viewed as a process rather than an event. Change is not automatically accomplished for the diocese or the parish by a mandate or a few workshops. Rather, change entails an unfolding of experience and a gradual development of skills. It is a developmental process which takes time.

A critical dimension of this process is the idea of Stages of Concern about the Change. Each Stage of Concern describes the feelings, perspectives, and attitudes of individual parishioners as they consider, approach and implement the change. The Stages of Concern move from early self-oriented concerns, to task-oriented concerns, to impact-oriented concerns. These seven stages are illustrated in Figure 1. Let us, however, first list the assumptions of this change process:

Change is:

1. a *process,* not an event.

2. made by *individual persons* first, then by the parish.

3. a highly *personal* experience.

4. entails *developmental growth* in feelings and skills.

5. focusing on *where the person (parishioner & pastor) is.*

Interventions must be related to:

1. the *people first.*

2. the *change second.*

Stages of Concern (Fig. 1)

Typical Expressions of Concern About the Change

Stages of Concern	*Expressions of Concern*
0 Awareness	I am not concerned about it (the change).
1 Informational	I would like to know more about it.
2 Personal	How will the change affect me?
3 Involvement	I seem to be spending all of my time working on this project.
4 Consequence	How will this change affect parishioners and priests?
5 Collaboration	I am interested in collaborating with people from neighboring parishes.
6 Refocusing	I have some ideas about some things that might work even better.

Levels of Activity of Parishes in Project (Fig. 2)

Typical Behaviors

Level of Activity	*Behaviors*
0 Inactivity	No activity is being taken on project.
1 Orientation	Parishioners are seeking out information about the project.
2 Preparation	Parishioners are preparing to implement the project.
3 Mechanical Use	Parishioners are organized to implement their goals and objectives.
4a Routine	Parishioners are making few or no changes and are continuing old routine.
4b Refinement	Parishioners are making visible changes.
5 Integration	Parishioners are making deliberate efforts to collaborate with neighboring parishes.
6 Renewal	Parishioners are seeking more effective alternatives to the established ways of administering, servicing, worshiping and educating.

Concerns-Based Interventions

Stage 0: (Awareness)

Parishioners in Stage 0 feel that the project does not concern them. They may have heard little about it. They do not feel that it will affect them. Typical statements may be: "I don't know anything about it." "I don't really want to know about it." "I have other concerns in my life right now."

Parish leaders may use the following interventions:

1. Acknowledge that little concern about the project is legitimate.

2. Share some information about the project in hopes of arousing some interest in it.

3. Tie the project to an area that the parishioner is _concerned about.

4. Encourage parishioners to talk with others about the project.

Stage 1: (Information)

Parishioners feel concerned about learning more about the project. Their concerns are general in nature. Typical statements may be: "I know a little about this and would like to know more." "I am interested in this, but I don't know enough to talk about it to any degree."

Parish Leaders may use the following interventions:

1. Share general descriptive information about the project through conversation, mailed brochures, or media.

2. Provide information contrasting what the parish is presently doing with what changes would entail.

3. Provide an opportunity to visit another parish where specific changes have been made.

4. Express a great deal of enthusiasm and involve others who are excited about what they have been doing in the parish or other parishes.

5. State realistic expectations about the benefits and costs associated with the intended changes.

Stage 2: (Personal)

Parishioners are indicating that, for whatever reason, they perceive the outcome of the project as a personal threat. In general, persons with intense concerns at this stage have doubts and uncertainty. Valid or invalid, these concerns are very real to the parishioners.

Parish leaders may use the following interventions:

1. Establish rapport and show signs of encouragement and assurance of personal adequacy such as through personal conversations or notes or homily reassurances.

2. Encourage implementation of changes gingerly; do not push unnecessarily.

3. Clarify how the project is related to other priorities that are potential conflicts in terms of energy and time demands.

4. Show how the project can be implemented by gradual introduction rather than with a major, all-encompassing leap (set reasonable, easy-to-meet expectations).

5. Provide personal support through easy access to the change facilitators or others who can be supportive and of assistance in use of the project workbook and materials.

6. Legitimize the expression of personal concerns.

Stage 3: (Involvement)

Involvement in the project makes people concerned about how they are managing the process of the project. Stage 3 concerns focus on the coordination, logistics and time that is used. Typical expressions might be: "It takes up too much of my time." "There are other things that I must do."

Parish leaders may use the following interventions:

1. The change agents should focus on the "how-to-do-its."

2. Acknowledge the appropriateness of management concern; offer assurance that they can be resolved.

3. Provide answers in ways that easily address the small specific "how-to" issues that are causes of concern.

4. Provide "hands on" material for people.

5. Do planning on one specific task and complete it.

6. Have others share information about the successful and unsuccessful practices.

7. Establish support groups.

8. Set a timeline for accomplishments of relatively simple and specific tasks.

Stage 4: (Consequences)

At this stage, parishioners are concerned about how the changes will affect them and the parish. Typical expressions may be: "I wonder how the proposed changes will affect our parish family." "I am finding that the more involved parishioners become in the project that they are supplying better quality suggestions."

People in Stage 4 are the ones with whom it is a pleasure to work. Their concerns are targeted toward individual persons and the quality of the proposed change.

Parish leaders may use the following interventions:

1. Regularly encourage and reinforce.

2. Send written information about topics that may be of interest.

3. Identify the parishioner's potential for sharing skills with others.

4. Send the person to a conference or a workshop on the topic to explain their skills to others or to refine their use.

Stage 5: (Collaboration)

Parishioners with intense Stage 5 collaboration concerns are rather rare. Most people would indicate that they are too busy with their own parish concerns to become involved with people from other parishes. Typical expressions of people who want to collaborate may be: "If I knew what other parishes were doing I could do a great service of informing our parishioners in order for us to be a better parish." "I have found that by working with people from neighboring parishes that collectively we have more power to help more people." People in Stage 5 end up being the leaders.

Parish leaders may use the following interventions:

1. Arrange meetings between the interested individuals.

2. Use Stage 5 people to help others through the process.

3. Bring in experts to help parishioners develop skills and resources in collaborative efforts.

4. Create opportunities for Stage 5 parishioners to circulate outside their parish and work with others who may be less knowledgeable.

Stage 6: (Refocusing)

People in Stage 6 indicate that they have alternative ideas and approaches which might have more impact than the proposed changes. Typical expressions may be: "I have some ideas about another way to do this." "The proposed changes have some clear weaknesses. I think that these weaknesses must be addressed. Maybe we could include these components."

Parish leaders may use the following interventions:

People in Stage 6 are self-starters and have their own goals. The following interventions can be used to help them focus on the limits within which they can deviate from the mainstream.

1. Help these parishioners focus energy into a productive direction for themselves and others.

2. Involve these parishioners as trainers of others.

3. Encourage these parishioners to take action with respect to their concerns.

Appendix E

Adult Learning and the Process of Change

A parish change project that emphasizes the inclusion and participation of adults in learning what the future societal and demographic trends are, how they might affect their parish, and what changes need to be made means that adults have to learn new skills and processes to deal adequately with the changing environment and the needs of parishioners. In order to help parish leaders more easily understand how they can create the proper conditions for adults to learn these skills, processes and new concepts, it would be helpful for them to know some basic assumptions about how adults learn best, and how adults can learn to cope with change. The key words are "learn" and "change."

Adult learning is usually called "andragogy" which is the art and science of helping adults learn. It deals with learning in a context of an individual's life experiences and the situation he/she finds himself in at the present moment. In 1926 Linderman provided basic assumptions about adult learners. They continue to be the foundation stones for modern adult learning ideas. These assumptions are:

1. Adult men and women are motivated to learn as they experience changing needs and interests; consequently, their needs and interests are the appropriate starting points for organizing adult learning activities.

2. Orientation to learning is life-centered for adults; consequently, life situations, not subject areas, are the appropriate units for organizing adult learning.

3. Adults find that experience is the richest resource for their learning; consequently, the analysis of their experience is the core methodology in their learning.

4. Adults prefer to be self-directing in their life-styles.

Consequently, the teacher's role is to engage the adult learner in a process of mutual discussion and inquiry, rather than to give them knowledge through lecturing and then evaluating the amount of their acquired knowledge.

5. The aging process increases the individual differences among adults. Consequently, teachers of adults must accommodate their differences in style, time, place, and pace of learning.

Based on the above assumptions Malcolm Knowles identified four major characteristics of the adult learning environment that must be considered when plans are being made to teach adults. This learning environment must be considered when men and women are invited to learn leadership skills, and when they are empowered to develop a plan of action for parish reorganization.

1. The adult's unique personality must be respected.

2. The adult learner must be included in decision making.

3. The adult learner must be allowed to freely express his/her opinions and must be given all relevant information.

4. In the adult learning environment, parishioners must be given opportunities for mutual responsibility, defining goals, planning and implementing action plans, and for appropriate evaluation.

In addition to the basic assumptions and major characteristics of adult learning, we can list two adult learning principles and five paradoxes that may be of some help to parish leaders as they try to assist adults in learning how to learn, and in learning how to adapt themselves and their parish structures to needed change.

Learning Principles

1. As adults learn, they need to be able to cope with the paradox of change. This is a situation where change and stability, dependency, interdependency and independency are all required. In these situations, adults need skills to ask questions appropriately, to address problems and solve them, to know how to be open to new ideas, and the ability to participate in decision making. A parish facilitator must be ready, willing and capable *to lead* parishioners through these processes. The facilitator must also possess an attitude of flexibility, a tolerance for ambiguity, diversity, and inconsistency in people. The facilitator cannot become defensive or angry when adult learners begin to emote their genuine feelings.

2. Adult learners (parishioners) who are being asked to consider change may respond to ambiguity and instability with anger, frustration and self-defense. The science of andragogy considers ambiguity and instability as necessary for adult learning. Therefore, anger will most likely be a fundamental component of adult learning.

Three Paradoxes in Adult Learning

1. The first paradox is the ability to maintain a balance between stability and change. Internal and external sources produce pressures for change. An adult can maintain a sense of stability by initiating change both in his own behavior and in the parish organization. To achieve stability, the individual parishioner must change; and, in order to achieve change, the parishioner must experience and respond to uncertainty and instability.

2. The second paradox is that individual parishioners will only achieve the needed change when they permit themselves to be vulnerable to the possibility of failure and the loss of self-esteem. If an individual or a parish (a group of individuals) explicitly or implicitly decide to avoid the threat of failure by not responding to the pressures for change, they expose themselves to other threats and dangers: stagnation, irrelevancy, ineffectiveness, obsolescence.

3. Another paradox exists when some parish leaders actually learn new or updated ideas, skills, processes and values. They can become more skilled, knowledgeable and competent than other parishioners and their at-

tempts to lead the parish into change efforts may endanger their personal relationships with others.

The steps and procedures, strategies and plans of action that have been outlined in this book have been structured and developed with full knowledge of the paradoxes of adult learning and based on the assumptions and principles of adult learning. It is with confidence, then, that we believe that any change effort attempted by parishes and dioceses which are guided by this book's Leadership Paradigm will be successful.

Notes

Introduction

1. Jerry Patterson, et al., Alexandria, Va 1986, 118.

2. John McKenzie, Milwaukee 1965, 231.

Chapter 1

1. Bishops' Committee on Priestly Life and Ministry, National Conference of Catholic Bishops, Washington, D.C., 1.

2. Ibid., 8.

3. Ibid., 15.

4. Ibid., 25.

5. Ibid., 32.

6. Ibid., 41.

7. Ibid., 41.

8. Ibid., 49.

9. J. Naisbitt, New York 1982, 23.

10. Donna Markham, New York 1984, 28.

11. Robert K. Greenleaf, New York 1977, 1.

12. Warren G. Bennis, New York 1982, 43.

13. Avery Dulles, New York 1974, 4.

14. Ibid., 208.

15. Greenleaf, 236-237.

16. Walbert Buhlmann, New York 1978, 200.

17. William Ouchi, London 1981, 43.

18. De Ecclesia, 8.

19. Joseph Gremillion & Jim Castelli, Notre Dame 1987, 75.

20. Ibid., 75.

21. Ibid., 75.

22. Ibid., 76.

23. Ibid., 76.

24. Ibid., 76.

25. Ibid., 76.

26. Ibid., 199.

Chapter 2

1. T.F. Omeara, Notre Dame 1982, 74.
2. Dulles, 17.
3. Hans Kung, 1967, 93.
4. Walter Abbot, ed., New York 1966, 30.

Chapter 3

1. Evelyn Whitehead and James Whitehead, New York 1982, 32.
2. Edward K. Braxton, New York May 22, 1985, 395.
3. Robert K. Greenleaf, New York 1977, 63-65.
4. Robert K. Greenleaf, New Hampshire 1972, 1-2.

Chapter 4

1. James MacGregor Burns, New York 1978, 462.
2. Decree on the Apostolate of the Laity, #3.
3. Leonardo Boff, New York 1985, 160.
4. Decree on the Apostolate of the Laity, #30.
5. Isabel Briggs Myers, Palo Alto 1962, A-4.
6. Avery Dulles, New York 1974, 200.
7. Ibid., 16.

Chapter 5

1. Kennedy Directory, Illinois 1988.
2. Philip Selznick, New York 1957, 28.
3. Thomas Watson, New York 1963, 4-6.
4. Alfred A. McBride, Washington, D.C., 14
5. Richard Pascale and Anthony Athos, New York 1981, 190.
6. Robert F. Taft, New Jersey 34.
7. Donald Nicholl, New York 1981, 6.
8. Lumen Gentium, #40.

Chapter 6

1. Jurgen Moltmann, New York 1976, xv.
2. Robert S. Hosmon and Gene Montague, New Jersey 1973, 18.
3. Richard E. Byrd, Massachussets 1987, 38.

4. John L. McKenzie, Milwaukee 1965, 84-85.

5. Robert K. Greenleaf, New York 1977, 227, 237.

6. Stephen B. Clark, Notre Dame, Indiana 1972, 98 & 104.

7. Rembert Weakland, NCR, 1988, 20.

8. Evelyn Whitehead and James Whitehead, New York 1982, 60.

9. John L. McKenzie, Milwaukee 1965, 152.

10. De Ecclesia, New Jersey 1964, #8.

Chapter 7

1. Warren G. Bennis, New York 1985, 31.

2. Greenleaf, New Jersey, 41-42.

3. Warren G. Bennis, New York 1985, 65.

4. R. Likert, New York 1961, 101.

5. John A. Shtogren 1980, 113.

6. Leonardo Boff, New York 1985, 57.

7. Ibid., 59.

8. Tad Guzie and Noreen Monroe Guzie, Mississippi 1984, 9.

9. Eric Fromm, New York 1956, 21.

10. Ibid., 22.

11. Ibid., 23.

12. Ibid., 24.

13. Ibid., 27.

14. On Evangelization in the Modern World, New York 1976, 48.

15. Bishop Howard J. Hubbard, Washington, D.C. 1978, 9.

16. Joseph Gremillion & Jim Castelli, San Francisco 1987, 27-28.

17. Bishop Howard J. Hubbard, Washington, D.C. 1978, 9.

Chapter 8

1. Richard McBrien, San Francisco 1987, 8.

2. Eric Fromm, New York 1956, 60.

3. The Constitution on the Church in the Modern World (GS45).

4. Evelyn Whitehead, & James Whitehead, New York 1982, 27.

5. Joseph Gremillion & Jim Castelli, San Francisco 1987, 27.

6. Walter Abbot, ed., New York 1966, 350.

Chapter 9

1. Isabel Briggs Myers, Palo Alto 1962, A-5.
2. John Shtogren, Texas 1980, 418.
3. Ibid., 420.
4. Ibid., 420.
5. Richard R. Broholm, Newton Centre, MA 1985, 134.
6. Ibid., 134.

Chapter 10

1. Weston H. Agor, New Jersey 1984, 5.
2. Peters and Waterman, New York 1982, 121.
3. Ibid., 131.

Appendix D

1. Hall, Wallace and Dossett, Texas 1973.

Bibliography

Abbot, Walter M., ed.: *The Documents of Vatican II*. New York: Herder & Herder, 1966.

Agor, Weston H.: *Intuitive Management*. New Jersey: Prentice Hall, 1984.

Argyris, C.: *Interpersonal Competence and Organizational Effectiveness*. Homewood, Illinois, 1962.

Beckhard, Richard: *Organization Development: Strategies and Models*. Reading, Massachusetts, 1969.

Bennis, Warren and Naus, Burt: *Leaders*. New York: Harper & Row, Publishers, Inc., 1985.

Bennis, Warren: *The Unconscious Conspiracy: Why Leaders Can't Lead*. New York: AMACOM, 1976.

Bishops' Committee on Priestly Life and Ministry, National Conference of Catholic Bishops: *A Shepherd's Care: Reflections on the Changing role of Pastor*. Washington, D.C.: United States Catholic Conference, Inc., 1987.

Blake, R.R., & Mouton, J.S.: *The Managerial Grid*. Houston: Gulf Publishing Co., 1964.

Boff, Leonardo: *Church, Charism & Power:* New York. Crossroad, 1985.

Braxton, Edward K.: *America,* 1985.

Broholm, Richard R.: *The Laity in Ministry*. Newton Centre, MA: The Robert K. Greenleaf Center, 1985.

Buhlmann, Walbert: *The Coming of the Third Church*. New York: Orbis Books, 1978.

Burns, James MacGregor: *Leadership*. New York: Harper & Row, Publishers, 1978.

Byrd, Richard E.: *Corporate Leadership Skills: A New Synthesis*. Newton Centre, MA: The Robert K. Greenleaf Center, 1987.

Clark, Stephen B.: *Building Christian Communities*. Notre Dame, Indiana: Ave Maria Press, 1972.

Cooke, Bernard: *Ministry to Word and Sacraments*. Philadelphia: Fortress Press, 1976.

De Chardin, Pierre Teilhard, *Toward the Future*. New York: Harcourt Brace Jovanovich, 1973.

Doohan, Helen: *Leadership in Paul*. Wilmington, Delaware: Michael Glazier, Inc., 1984.

Downs, Thomas: *The Parish As Learning Community*. New York: Paulist Press, 1979.

Drucker, Peter F.: *Managing in Turbulent Times*. New York: Harper & Row, Publishers, 1980.

Dulles, Avery: *A Church to Believe In*. New York: The Crossroad Publishing Co., 1982.

____ *Models of the Church*. New York: Image Books, Doubleday & Co., Inc., 1978.

Foley, Gerald: *Empowering the Laity*. Kansas City, MO: Sheed & Ward, 1986.

Fromm, Eric: *The Art of Loving*. New York: Harper & Row, Publishers, 1956.

Garvey, John, ed.: *Modern Spirituality: an Anthology*. Springfield, Illinois: Templegate Publishers, 1985.

Greeley, Andrew: *What a Modern Catholic Believes About the Church*. Chicago: The Thomas More Press, 1972.

Greenleaf, Robert K.: *The Institution as Servant*. Peterborough, N.H.: Windy Row Press, 1972.

_____ *Servant Leadership*. New York: Paulist Press, 1977.

Gremillion, Joseph, and Castelli, Jim: *The Emerging Parish*. San Francisco Harper & Row, Publishers, 1987.

Guzie, Tad and Guzie, Noreen Monroe: Journal of Psychological Type, Volume 7, *Masculine and Feminine Archetypes: A Complement to the Psychological Types*, 1984.

Hall, Gene, et al.: *CBAM Project*. Washington, D.C.: NIE, 1973.

Hanline, C. Jeanne: *The Official Catholic Directory,* Macmillan Directory Division, Wilmette, Illinois, 1988.

Hersey, Paul and Blanchard, Kenneth H.: *Management of Organizational Behavior: Utilizing Human Resources,* 3rd edition. New Jersey: Prentice-Hall, Inc., 1977.

Herskovits, Melville J.: *Cultural Dynamics*. New York: Alfred A. Knopf, Inc., 1967.

Hosmon, Robert and Montague, Gene: *Man: Paradox and Promise*. New Jersey: Prentice Hall, 1973.

Hubbard, Bishop Howard J.: *The Vision: We Are His People: A Pastoral Letter*. Washington, D.C.: United States Catholic Conference, 1978.

Ivory, Thomas P.: *Conversion and Community*. New York: Paulist Press, 1988.

Jung, C.G.: *Psychological types*. New York: Harcourt, Brace, 1923.

Jung, C.G.: *Psychological types*. Bollingen Series XX. The Collected Works of C.G. Jung, vol. 6. Princeton: Princeton University Press, 1971.

Keirsey, David and Bates, Marilyn: *Please Understand Me*. Del Mar, California: Promethean Books, Inc., 1978.

Kibler, Robert J., Barker, Larry L., and Miles, David T.: *Behavioral Objectives and Instruction*. Boston: Allyn and Bacon, Inc., 1970.

Knowles, Malcolm S.: *The Modern Practice of Adult Education*. Chicago: Association Press, Follett Publishing Company, 1980.

Kuhn T.S.: *The Structure of Scientific Revolutions*. Chicago: University Press, 1970.

Küng, Hans: *The Church*. New York: Sheed and Ward, 1967.

Lawrence, Gordon: *People Types & Tiger Stripes,* Second Edition. Gainesville, Florida: Published by Center for Applications of Psychological Type, Inc., 1979.

Leithwood, K.A., Holmes, M., and Montgomery, D.J.: *Helping Schools Change.* Ontario: The Ontario Institute for Studies in Education, 1979.

Likert, R.: *New Patterns of Management.* New York: McGraw-Hill, 1961.

Markham, Donna: *Human Development: Psychological Aspects of Change.* Volume Five, Number Three, Fall, New York: Le Jacq Publishing Inc., 1984.

McBride, Alfred A.: *The Christian Formation of Catholic Educators, A CACE Monograph.* Washington, D.C.: Published by the Chief Administrators of Catholic Education, 1981.

McBrien, Richard P.: *Ministry.* San Francisco: Harper & Row, Publishers, 1987.

McKenzie, John L.: *The Power and the Wisdom.* Milwaukee: The Bruce Publishing Company, 1965.

Moltmann, Jurgen: *The Theology of Hope.* New York: Harper and Row, Publishers Inc., 1976.

Myers, Isabel Briggs: *Introduction to Type.* Palo Alto: Consulting Psychologists Press, Inc., 1962

Myers, Isabel Briggs: *Gifts Differing.* Palo Alto: Consulting Psychologists Press, Inc., 1980.

Naisbitt, John: *Megatrends.* New York: Warner Books, 1982.

Nicholl, Donald: *Holiness.* New York: The Seabury Press, 1981.

O'Grady, John F.: *Models of Jesus.* New York: Doubleday & Co., 1981.

O'Meara, T.F.: *Romantic Idealism & Roman Catholicism.* Notre Dame: University of Notre Dame Press, 1982.

Ouchi, William: *Theory Z.* Reading, Massachusetts: Addison-Wesley Publishing Company, 1981.

Pascale, Richard Tanner and Athos, Anthony G.: *The Art of Japanese Management.* New York: Simon & Schuster, 1981.

Patterson, Jerry L., Purkey, Stewart C., and Parkers, Jackson V.: *Productive School Systems For A Nonrational World.* Alexandria, Va.: Association for Supervision and Curriculum Development, 1986.

Peters, Edward: *De Ecclesia, The Constitution on the Church,* New Jersey: Deus Books, Paulist Press, 1964.

Peters, Thomas J. and Waterman, Robert H., Jr.: *In Search of Excellence.* New York: Harper & Row, Publishers, 1982.

Peterson, Betty Dillon: *Staff Development/Organization Development.* Alexandria, Va.: Association for Supervision and Curriculum Development.

Provost, James H., ed.: *Code, Community, Ministry.* Washington, D.C.: Canon Law Society of America, 1983.

Rademacher, with Rogers, Marliss: *The New Practical Guide for Parish Councils.* Mystic, Connecticut: Twenty-Third Publications, 1988.

Sarason, Seymour B.: *The Culture of the School and the Problem of Change.* Boston: Allyn and Bacon, Inc., 1971.

Selznick, Philip: *Leadership in Administration: A Sociological Interpretation.* New York: Harper & Row, 1957.

Schillebeeckx, Edward: *The Church With A Human Face.* New York: Crossroad, 1987.

Shtogren, John A.: *Models for Management: The Structure of Competence.* Teleometrics Int'l, Woodlands, Texas, 1980.

Silver, Michael: *Values Education.* Washington, D.C.: National Education Association, 1976.

Taft, Robert F.: *Eastern Rite Catholicism, Its Heritage and Vocation.* New Jersey: Paulist Press, 1963.

Wallace, Walter L., ed.: *Sociological Theory.* Chicago: Aldine Publishing Company, 1969.

Weakland, Rembert: National Catholic Reporter, 1988.

Watson, Thomas J. Jr.: *A Business and Its Believers: The Ideas That Helped Build IBM.* New York: McGraw Hill, 1963.

Whitehead, Evelyn and Whitehead, James: *Community of Faith: Models and Strategies for Developing Christian Communities.* The Seabury Press, New York: 1982.

Wiles, Kimvall and Lovell, John T.: *Supervision for Better Schools.* New Jersey: Prentice-Hall, 1975.